W9-CSB-195

Copyright 2008
Hicklin Galleries, LLC/The Charleston Renaissance Gallery
103 Church Street · Charleston, South Carolina 29401
843.723.0025 · fineartsouth.com

Spot: Southern Works on Paper
Editor: Lynne Blackman
Essay, "Drawing the South:" Philip L. Brewer, M.D.
Foreword: Robert M. Hicklin, Jr.
Preface: Roberta Sokolitz
Catalogue entries: Roberta Sokolitz (RS); Valerie Ann Leeds (VAL); Nancy Rivard Shaw (NRS);
Alexander Moore (AM); and Estill Curtis Pennington (ECP)
Assistant Editor: Holly Watters
Design: Gee Creative
Photography: Rick Rhodes

Library of Congress Cataloging-in-Publication Data

Spot : southern works on paper : the Charleston Renaissance Gallery, Charleston, South Carolina /
[editor, Lynne Blackman ; essay, Philip L. Brewer ; foreword, Robert M. Hicklin, Jr. ; preface,
Roberta Sokolitz ; catalogue entries, Roberta Sokolitz ... et al.].

    p. cm.

Catalog of an exhibition to be held at the Charleston Renaissance Gallery, Charleston, S.C.,
between Nov. 7 and Dec. 31, 2008.

Includes index.

ISBN 0-9785365-2-5

1. Watercolor painting, American–Southern States—Exhibitions.
2. Drawing, American—Southern States—Exhibitions.
3. Watercolor painting—South Carolina—Charleston–Exhibitions.
4. Drawing—South Carolina—Charleston—Exhibitions.
5. Charleston Renaissance Gallery (Charleston, S.C.)—Exhibitions.
I. Blackman, Lynne.
II. Brewer, Philip L.
III. Charleston Renaissance Gallery (Charleston, S.C.)

ND1811.S69 2008

759.15074'757915—hdc22

                                                                            2008035139

On the cover: Nicolino Vicompte Calyo (1799-1884), *View of New Orleans*, circa 1852,
watercolor and gouache on paper, 5 x 7¾ inches.

This spread: Patrick Henry Bruce (1881-1937), *Live Oak* (detail), pastel on paper, 16 x 20 inches.

table of contents

Stephen Scott Young (born 1957), *Woodward's Café*, 1993, pencil on paper, 18 x 18 inches, signed lower right: *Woodward Cafe/Spartanburg SC/28 May 93/S S Young*. Inscribed lower left: *South Carolina/ Breakfast/Spartanburg Chicken and Eggs and 'Baby' Cokes.*

foreword

I DO NOT KNOW WHAT ECONOMY GETTING DOUBLE DUTY FROM A name might represent. When the connection is, however, more of a dichotomy than an entendre, we can only catch credence on the sly. Maybe it is only in my mind that it all comes together.

Fully half the art dealers in New York—and many others from across America and distant shores—have shared an artery-clogging meal of the best damn fried chicken at a small, cramped house on Spartanburg, South Carolina's west side, a place called Woodward's Cafe. In business since 1926, Woodward's stood unrivaled as the best out-of-the-way place at the end of a less-traveled road this man—who traveled so much in the pursuit of Southern art and those who sold, collected, and wrote about it—knew. The noted watercolorist Stephen Scott Young and his dealer, John Surovek, came to the Upstate to call on Tom Styron at the Greenville County Museum one day in 1993. It was my pleasure to pick them up at the airport. When they both reported that they were hungry after the morning's flight—and with Scott's choice of subject matter in mind—we turned toward Spartanburg and breakfast at Woodward's. We all had the fried chicken as a side to grits and eggs. That chicken was so thoroughly enjoyed and fussed over that when lunch time came, Scott found a sketchpad and pencils and asked to return. Charles Whitmire, "Spot" to his friends and regulars, was just a little leery, but he had surely seen it all before. One of the sketches Scott made that day is shown here.

If a drawing is born from a line and a line is born from, well, the first contact between pencil and paper, I suppose one could say it all begins with a spot. Scott Young was moved by the honesty of the place to record what he saw, though memory of the chicken surely had something to do with it. Each of the works in this catalogue shares something of that. The innate vitality of on-the-spot creations—ranging from Calyo's rendering of Natchez to Charles Shannon's highly-charged *Syncopation Number 2*—grows from that same first contact between the pencil or the brush and the surface on which we view the picture today.

Those who dined with me at Woodward's still talk about the chicken whenever we talk art. Amazing—what a simple, shared meal can lead to, including much of the feast that follows. All beginning with a spot.

Robert M. Hicklin, Jr.

preface

THIS CATALOGUE FOLLOWS IN THE LEGACY OF JAMES C. KELLY'S *The South on Paper: Line, Color, and Light*, published by Rob Hicklin in 1985. As an art historian and publications director for the Gibbes Museum in the 1980s, I often went to that volume as a first-hand reference and research book, especially valuable for concise and scholarly content, biographies, and sources. Then, it was one of only a few comprehensive surveys of Southern art, and the book contributed regularly toward my understanding of this subject as a particular regionalism, rich in currents and connections with people, culture, history, and nature.

Today, the field of Southern art history is extensively documented on many levels and continues to grow through the efforts of museums, experts, dealers, collectors, and audiences. And no wonder, given the diversity and depth of the material, and the South's reverence for and preservation of history.

This exceptional group of original works on paper traces European-American artistic traditions of drawing, watercolors, and gouache, dating from the early nineteenth century picturesque to contemporary post-modernism. Foremost among the treasures represented here is Joshua Shaw's *Natural Bridge No. 1*, one of eight original (circa 1820) oil sketches and paintings of Virginia and the Carolinas by this noted English-American landscape artist, that have come to light only in the past two years. As a group, these views and their accompanying manuscript descriptions significantly help to revise and enrich our understanding of Southern landscape art.

Dr. Philip Brewer speaks of the delight of such discoveries in his fine essay, intelligently guiding us with his observations on evolving styles and genres, including topographical, figurative, classical, impressionistic, and modern. He brings the experienced eye of a collector and connoisseur to his understanding of the art, and the insights of a native Southerner to his observations on regionalism. My talented colleagues, Valerie Ann Leeds and Nancy Rivard Shaw, worked diligently to research and write most of the catalogue entries here—they too often marveling about what they had learned and discovered in the process. Alexander D. Moore and Estill Curtis Pennington likewise shared their enthusiasm and expertise in selected entries. Lynne Blackman exquisitely refined and organized the entire volume and, together with Holly Watters, managed the demanding details related to text, imagery, and production.

In his foreword, Rob Hicklin, who acquired these outstanding works over several decades, reflects that a drawing does in fact begin from a "spot" made with pencil, pen, watercolor, or other medium on paper. At the same time, he reminds us how much of Southern culture is about connections that can happen anywhere, at any time, whether over a shared meal at a humble diner or in study and conversation over a priceless Southern masterwork.

Roberta Sokolitz

Joshua Shaw (1777-1860), *Natural Bridge No. 1,* circa 1820, oil on paper on panel, 6¾ x 9¾ inches.

drawing the south

Philip L. Brewer, M.D.

beginnings

ROB HICKLIN, IN HIS WONDERFULLY AUTOBIOGRAPHICAL essay "Blackberry Winter," describes his discovery, thirty-five years ago, of a drawing, the subject of which he immediately recognized as the historic Eagle and Phenix Mill in Columbus, Georgia.[1] Born in Columbus to a father who began a lengthy career in the textile industry in that very mill, Rob made the fortuitous purchase in New York City, operating on borrowed funds and little more than the happy recognition of something familiar and Southern. His acquisition of the picture from Kennedy Galleries and the subsequent purchase of the drawing for the Columbus Museum are cited as turning points which prompted his career in art, a career that has established him as the preeminent dealer in art of the American South.

American, unknown artist, *Eagle and Phenix Mills, Columbus, Georgia*, circa 1870s, watercolor on wove paper, 9½ x 13 inches. Collection of the Columbus Museum, Columbus, Georgia; Gift of G. Gunby Jordan for the Museum's Silver Anniversary. 77.43.

I found this story to be doubly interesting because Columbus, Rob's birthplace, is also my hometown. Columbus is one of many Southern cities located along the fall line, a broad crescent extending south from Virginia, then across the Carolinas and Georgia, and into Alabama and Mississippi. This line marks the transition from rolling Piedmont hills to flat coastal plain. Below this line, gently flowing rivers are navigable to the sea and here small communities grew up throughout the South. Beginning in the late nineteenth century, the rivers offered a source of hydroelectric power. Power and cheap labor, abundant in the South from the time of Reconstruction through the Great Depression, provided the basis for the cotton mill industry and earned such enclaves the pejorative appellation, "mill towns." Not until the latter twentieth century did these cities experience economic growth commensurate with the rest of the country.

More interesting to me personally was learning that Rob had discovered the picture at Kennedy Galleries, where I too, in the early 1970s, purchased my first work of art on paper. In those early days, one could walk into their street-level Manhattan gallery and rummage through a bin of cellophane-wrapped drawings and watercolors, each priced at a few hundred dollars. Today, these same works, elaborately framed, hang secured on gallery walls, their value appreciated by dealers and collectors alike.

What is it about these drawings, or about any fine works on paper, that attracts us and why do they give us so much pleasure?

I consider it noteworthy that Rob, at this earliest point in his career, chose to buy and sell a drawing, rather than an oil painting. Admittedly, financial considerations helped to dictate his choice, but, nevertheless, his commitment to drawings has continued to include this, his second exhibition of works on paper with a companion catalogue. Fine Southern drawings of the kind Rob favors—his "period pieces"—are rare. While in recent years, his Charleston Renaissance Gallery has added several talented contemporary artists, I count only four in this assemblage who were born after 1950. As such, it remains largely a document of the historic South.[2] To search out drawings of such high quality and to have done so over the course of nearly four decades is a remarkable achievement, one that requires an educated eye—and a nose.

What is it about these drawings, or about any fine works on paper, that attracts us and why do they give us so much pleasure?[3] If you would like to witness magic, watch a master draughtsman see the subjects that you see, filter them through his mind's eye,

and then make them reappear on a sheet of paper. Realize, of course, that what you are watching requires not only genius, but long hours of thoughtful practice. The simplicity of the tools with which he works frees him and allows spontaneity. Little wonder, for example, that a preliminary portrait sketch often captures the personality of the subject in a way that the finished product does not. As you train your eye, subtleties will appear. The strength or delicacy of a line will vary with the amount of pressure placed on the drawing instrument. Strokes may be short and nervous or long and languid as befits the subject. The artist may enclose his subject within lines, as with a contour drawing, or use a gestural method to indicate attitude or movement. You may even be able to tell by the slant of the line whether the artist is left-handed or right-handed.

Observe how well a watercolorist controls his washes and whether he applies opaque pigment (gouache) for his highlights or lets the brightness of the paper shine through. Notice the paper: it may be thick, thin, tinted, or colorless. Different effects will be produced when a brush or crayon is dragged across the surface of a sheet, depending on the roughness (tooth) of the paper and whether the paper is flat (wove) or patterned (laid).[4]

Consider the technique of Alice Ravenel Huger Smith, a self-trained artist who was a major figure in the Charleston Renaissance art movement, as described by a friend.

Above left: Milton Avery (1893-1965), *Nude on a Chair*, circa 1948-1950, brown and black marker on wove paper, 17 x 14 inches. Collection of the Columbus Museum, Columbus, Georgia; Dr. and Mrs. Philip L. Brewer Collection, Museum purchase made possible by the Ella E. Kirven Charitable Lead Trust for Acquisitions. 2003.1.10. © 2008 Milton Avery Trust / Artists Rights Society (ARS), New York.

Above right: William Morris Hunt (1824-1879), *Figure on a Horse*, circa 1855-1860; on verso: *Woman with Pail*, lithographic crayon on wove paper; Collection of the Columbus Museum, Columbus, Georgia; Gift of Dr. and Mrs. Theodore Stebbins, Jr. 2004.21.2.

"When she painted she wet the entire surface of the board first . . . [and then] added the colors of the sky, water, etc. . . . [Only] a relatively small part of any painting is conventionally painted [on a dry surface] with a wet brush."[5] These watercolor techniques are basic, wet on wet and wet on dry, and yet Smith's results were unique watercolor poems to the Carolina Lowcountry.

Few would believe that an illustration of an oil painting, with its impastos made by a brush or pallet knife, could be an adequate substitute for actually looking at the painting itself. Yet many assume, incorrectly, that viewing a reproduction suffices for evaluating a work of art on paper. Only by seeing the image first-hand can the fine points, just a few of which are mentioned above, be appreciated.

the collection

The scope of this collection accommodates a variety of interests. Some viewers will appreciate the documentary nature of a scene of the siege of Petersburg or a sketch of Daniel Webster, yet there is an overriding aesthetic appeal as well. Topographical watercolor views, popular in the nineteenth century, are included with examples by J. W. Champney (*View of Norfolk, Virginia*, 1873); Rudolf Cronau (*A Cotton Plantation in South Carolina*, 1891); W. H. Dougal (three 1889 views of Washington, D.C.); and the peripatetic Neapolitan Nicolino Calyo (mid-century views of New Orleans, Cincinnati, and the bluffs at Natchez). The Calyo drawing of New Orleans, a small gem painted in gouache, shows the city from the west bank of the Mississippi River. Calyo captured not only the topography of the city, but has added local flavor by including two dandies in frock coats, three laborers with their straw plantation hats, and a woman carrying sugar cane. A charming but out-of-scale paddle-wheeler flies a prominent American flag.

William H. Dougal (1822-1895), *View from North End of 16th Street, Washington, D.C.*, 1889, watercolor on paper, 3⅜ x 14 inches.

Equally as rare as the Calyo scene is the circa 1820 painting of the Natural Bridge in Virginia by one of America's earliest landscape artists, Joshua Shaw. Traditional depictions present the bridge from below, emphasizing the arch, the open space beneath it, and the sheer cliffs that descend to the bottom of the ravine. Shaw has chosen an unusual vantage point, showing us the surface of the bridge. A lone figure who cautiously approaches the edge of the precipice on hands and knees suggests what lies below.

Also an early work, *Georgia Pelican*, by the Englishman John Abbot (1751-1840) is a fine example of the art of ornithology, a tradition which culminated in the magnificent publications of John James Audubon. The drawing also attests to the intense interest of nineteenth century Europeans in the natural history of the New World.

The drawings by Catlin deserve special mention. His portraits of the two Indian chiefs, one a Creek and the other a Cherokee, were taken after the United States government removed them from their homes in Georgia and Alabama and sent them to the Arkansas and Oklahoma territories. Before their removal, Creek braves had been defeated at the Battle of Horseshoe Bend near Tallahassee, Alabama, a slaughter from which "no more than twenty" Indians survived.[6] The peaceful Cherokees, driven from their homes in the Carolinas into northwest Georgia, owned property and were deemed by Catlin to be "chiefly civilized and agricultural."[7] Despite vastly different attitudes toward their white neighbors, Creek and Cherokee alike were uprooted, stripped of their land, and forced to embark on the "Trail of Tears," where thousands died of hunger, cold, and infectious disease. Catlin, who portrays the Indians with a sure hand, has chosen to show the Creek warrior with his rifle, while, ironically, the Cherokee clutches his ineffectual peace pipe.

Peter Woltze, who worked in New Orleans, but about whom little else is known, displayed a remarkable technical facility in telling the stories of ordinary citizens.

John Mackie Falconer (1820-1903), *Portrait of a Seated Man*, 1853, watercolor on paper, 9½ x 6½ inches.

His drawing, (*Docks, New Orleans*, circa 1889), displays the miniaturist's gift for capturing the face of his subjects and identifying them as individuals. Also among these earlier works are the sketches of Xanthus Smith (*Scene on the Beaufort River*, circa 1863-1864) and Thomas Addison Richards (*Accabee, Ashley River, South Carolina*, 1852), possible memory aids for later paintings. Decidedly not a preliminary sketch is the finished watercolor, *Southern Scene*, by Frank English. He has included mules and moss—everything one could desire in a rural Southern setting—enlivened with touches of lapis. John Falconer, another watercolorist known to have worked in the Deep South, is represented by two mid-century figural drawings, *Portrait of a Seated Man* and *Portrait of a Man*.

The influence of French impressionism on twentieth century American art is so pervasive that pure examples of impressionist work as expressed on paper are difficult to single out. An exception might be Frank Benson's watercolor, *Dog River, Alabama*, which demonstrates his open air approach, use of the underlying brightness of the paper to mimic sunlight, and purple shadows. Best known for his impressionistic oil paintings of his wife and three daughters on sunny New England days, Benson was an avid sportsman who produced numerous watercolors of his favorite fishing spots, including this painting done near Mobile, Alabama. A second case in point is *Grazing* by Edward Middleton Manigault, who successfully translates the difficult and laborious task of adapting the broken strokes of the impressionist painters to watercolor. Hobson Pittman's pastel, *Moonlit Gardens—Cypress Gardens Near Charleston*, is also clearly inspired by impressionism. Pittman used only four colors—blue, gold, white, and black—to depict moonlight on a cypress swamp. The effect is scintillating. Finally, the impressionist painter William de Leftwich Dodge has given us a demonstration of his control over the watercolor medium in the large, fluid portrait of *Ezell's Brother*.

In the late nineteenth and early twentieth centuries, most of the revolutionary artistic movements of Europe failed to make inroads in the South.

Urbanization, industrialization, and immigration, the forces that changed the face of America in the late nineteenth and early twentieth centuries, were less pronounced in the South. Here, cities were smaller, industrial development lagged, and the spirit of the people remained agrarian. With few exceptions (notably, the Italians of New Orleans), the immigrants that swelled Northern cities did not find their way southward. Similarly, most of the revolutionary artistic movements of Europe failed to make inroads in the South. Alfred Stieglitz, the proselyte of modernism, opened his *291* gallery in New York. The influential Armory Show, after visiting New York, Boston, and Chicago, did not cross the Mason-Dixon Line. Not only did the impoverished South have few commercial galleries in which to show the new art, municipal museums were either underfunded or nonexistent. When exhibitions were held, they were sponsored by guilds, clubs, leagues, art centers, and art associations established by the artists and their patrons. A majority of the artists were native Southerners who had developed their skills away from home, most frequently at the Art Students League on New York's

Fifty-seventh Street, but also at the National Academy of Design, Pennsylvania Academy of the Fine Arts, Boston Museum of Fine Art, or Art Institute of Chicago. A smattering of students left the country to study in France or with the Mexican muralists. When they returned, these artists, though now familiar with Picasso, Cezanne, and Matisse, had rejected the more radical forms of modernism—perhaps as foreign, or even worse, Northern. Along with their customers, they preferred a more representational art, characterized by story-telling and the Southerner's legendary sense of place: in a word, regionalism. Regionalism—or, as it is now called, the American Scene—became the dominant theme in Southern art up to the end of World War II.[8]

Four compelling watercolors by Southern Scene artists Charles Shannon, Margaret Law, Anna Heyward Taylor, and Augusta Oelschig share an important commonality. Although all four pictures contain African American subjects, a prevalent theme throughout the collection, what unites these artists is that they delve beneath the superficial use of African Americans as elements of the picturesque. In Shannon's *Syncopation Number 1* (circa 1939), a small gouache with great impact, the preacher, Bible in hand, raises his arm in rhythmic jubilation. One can almost hear his shout and the congregation's enthusiastic reply. At his side, a figure at the piano adds to the sense of musicality. Vibrant color complements the scene, and, in some areas, white pigment mixed with black shines like silver leaf.

> Along with their customers, Southern artists preferred a more representational art, characterized by story-telling and a sense of place: in a word, regionalism.

The call and response of Africa is an even stronger element in Taylor's 1933 watercolor, *The Spiritual Society Dancing Scene*, in which figures dance and sing spirituals around an open fire. Taylor's painting is strikingly similar to *Spirituals in the Lowcountry*, a previously published watercolor by Alfred Hutty, and both pictures were said to have been painted on the same outing.[9] The Spiritual Society, properly called the Society for the Preservation of Spirituals, was founded in 1921 by city leaders in Charleston to educate the public concerning the "Negro Spiritual," unique American music that had grown out of slavery. Choral groups sponsored by the society performed along the East Coast before appreciative audiences and for dignitaries such as President Franklin Roosevelt.[10]

In contrast, labor, rather than religion, is the subject of *Harvest*, a watercolor by Law. Her brusque, no-nonsense style and strokes of pure color are perfectly in tune with her subject, a large woman picking vegetables. The woman's back is bent by time and the weight of the basket on her shoulder, but there is strength in her muscular forearms. We know that she could continue to work in that field long after others dropped from exhaustion.

Augusta Oelschig's powerful drawing, *Do Unto Others*, is reminiscent of the highly charged anti-lynching art of Paul Cadmus, John Stuart Curry, and others done two decades earlier. Executed around 1950—at the dawn of the Civil Rights movement—this work dates well beyond the peak incidence of lynching in the 1890s.[11] The victims lie in a crumpled heap. To our right stands a lone, hooded presence and, to the left, kneeling figures might represent the grief-stricken family or the guilt-ridden perpetrators. The artist's intention is to remind us, as Faulkner did, that the past is never really past.[12]

Alfred Hutty (1877-1954), *Spirituals in the Lowcountry*, circa 1933, watercolor on board, 5 x 6 inches, The Wright Southern Collection.

Corrie McCallum (born 1914), *Ft. Sumter, From a Contemporary Engraving*, 1961, watercolor and gouache on paper, 20½ x 26 inches.

Alfred Hutty, Kelly Fitzpatrick, and William Hollingsworth, also recognized Southern Scene painters, are represented by three watercolors. Hutty's *Wash Day, Charleston, S.C.*, circa 1920, demonstrates once again that he is a master at depicting the vernacular architecture of his adopted city. In *On the Lake, Alabama* of 1945, Fitzpatrick paints a sparkling body of water—possibly Lake Jordan, near Montgomery, where he established his Dixie Art Colony. Hollingsworth presents *Portrait of a Man, Jackson, Mississippi*, his subject blocked in with planes of black and brown. A native South Carolinian, Faith Cornish Murray offers a slightly more modern approach in *Among the Trees, Edisto Island*, a painting perhaps influenced by her teacher Arthur Wesley Dow.

A precisionist work may seem anomalous amidst these Southern Scene paintings, but the 1937 watercolor, *The Battery, Charleston, South Carolina*, by visiting artist Sandor Bernath eliminates details and concentrates on the broad shapes of the cannon. He also shows us his technical virtuosity, allowing pigment to bleed and capture the round and cylindrical tonalities.

Figure drawings by Walter Biggs, George Beattie, Jr., and Mabel May Woodward are included in the collection. In *Southern Scene*, Biggs portrays two opulently dressed gentlemen with a gentle humor, while *Woodward's Flower Ladies, Charleston*, circa 1935-1940, presents the city's iconic street vendors with pastel as colorful as the blossoms themselves. Beattie's *Tybee Island, Savannah, Georgia*, a drawing of a bemused young woman standing on a beach, suggests the robust sensuality of Reginald Marsh. Beattie has added interest with fine lines done in pen and ink, describing the fabric of her dress, the weathered piling beside her, and the strakes of a broken beach umbrella. To me, there is something unsettling about this composition, and it serves as a kind of memento mori.

The South has long held a fascination for visiting artists. Many of these came as illustrators, a profession known for draughtsmanship and for producing rapidly completed, fluid watercolors. This is evident in the work of two artists: Karl Oberteuffer's *Cocktail Bar, New Orleans*, circa 1935, and *Folly Beach S.C.* of 1926 by James Montgomery Flagg. Another visitor and competent watercolorist, William Lester Stevens, had no difficulty transposing his nostalgic formula for painting New England townships to the South. In *Charleston, South Carolina*, Stevens simply left out the elm trees. Quite different is the brooding pastel of an Edisto Island ruin by George Hand Wright. *Old Brick, Edisto Island, S.C., View of Creek*, circa 1915, evokes memories of glories past, much as the work of photographer Clarence John Laughlin did in his classic *Ghosts Along the Mississippi*.[13]

With the arrival of the second half of the twentieth century, the pace of social and economic change in the South accelerated, and her artists began to reflect an extraordinary diversity.

The late Paul Cummings, adjunct curator of drawing at the Whitney Museum of American Art, said "American drawings . . . differ in ambition, size, scale, color, imagery, and function from anything in the graphic tradition."[14] With the arrival of the second half of the twentieth century, the pace of social and economic change in the South accelerated, and her artists began to reflect the extraordinary diversity that Cummings suggests. One harbinger of these artistic advances was Will Henry Stevens, a professor at Sophie Newcomb College in New Orleans, who had been producing non-objective art since admiring Kandinsky in the 1930s. His *Woodlands* painting of 1943 reflects his masterful use of color and application of pastels in a way that created flowing organic forms.

The facades of buildings are the subjects of drawings by both Maltby Sykes and William Halsey, and it is instructive to consider these two artists together. Born in the second decade of the twentieth century, both "went up North" to learn to be artists—

Sykes to New York and Halsey to Boston—and both learned from the Mexican muralists. Upon returning home, their work was not unlike that of other Southern regionalists; by the 1950s, however, both artists were producing art that eventually evolved into pure abstraction. In *Facades, Charleston*, Halsey, the colorist, defines the forms of his buildings with planes of color, using lines incidentally to denote doors and windows Sykes, although he uses blocks of brown, black, and blue in *Sea Barns*, circa 1962-1969, seems conversely fascinated by line, which he draws in a meticulous but childlike fashion to delineate shingles, clapboard, and door hinges. The subjects are similar, but the artists, each committed to a modernist approach, produce results that are quite different. Halsey's wife Corrie McCallum is also represented with a 1961 watercolor of Fort Sumter.

Through these drawings and watercolors, artists tell of the last two hundred years of Southern history in distinctly personal ways.

The artist in this collection who comes closest to pure abstraction is Marie Hull. Executed with vigorous, expressive strokes, Hull's painting, circa 1955, is aptly titled *Sunburst*. Half a century later, Linda Fantuzzo has mixed hard-edged and nebulous strokes to take an everyday sight—a power station near her Charleston home—and create a mysterious, shimmering black tabernacle in *Electric Cathedral*.

Race looms large in the background of any discussion of the South. One needs look no further than the images in this catalogue to realize that African Americans are a prevailing presence in Southern art. Master watercolorist Stephen Scott Young has built his career on painting these subjects with care and sensitivity, as in *The Veterans* of 1993. Clint Herring, another watercolorist working in the realist tradition, has found character in the facade of a Charleston house in *Captain's Quarters* of 2005. The aging building's stains and missing balusters seem to reflect the wounds and scars of the inhabitants within. Drawn shades at the windows add to the sense of mystery.

Many of the works featured in this collection appeal to the Southerner's love of tradition. A parallel trait is Southerners' tolerance—some might say affection—for eccentricity. Tarleton Blackwell has created a mythology of the familiar. His paintings and drawings, based on the compositions of Velasquez, are inhabited by his own personal menagerie: hogs (as seen in the example included here, *Hog Series XLIX: Tractor/Maria Teresa*), opossums, roosters, and his dog Wolf. Unusual as well are the whimsical compositions of William Dunlap. Some paintings are panoramic Southern landscapes, but in others such as *Water Side—Iris Watch* of 2004, he places flowers or dogs against the Florida sunsets of Martin Johnson Heade. Blackwell and Dunlap are accomplished artists whose quirkiness only adds to their appeal.

A discussion of these last four artists seems to be an appropriate way to conclude this essay, considering their focus on the Southern land and the people and creatures who live here. Through the drawings and watercolors of this collection, artists tell of the last two hundred years of Southern history in distinctly personal ways. Encounters with Native Americans and with the natural world, slavery, King Cotton, a war in which over six hundred thousand Americans died, the poverty of Reconstruction, the awakening of Henry Grady's New South, agrarianism, civil rights, regionalism, and the late arrival of modernism: all are touched on. As to be expected in a collection limited by the availability of such rare material, much is necessarily omitted. Perhaps in a few years, Rob will present us with a third collection of works on paper by which more blanks will be filled in, but, inevitably, new questions are certain to be asked.

final thoughts

Like the rest of the country, the past century has wrought dramatic changes in the South—some for the better, some for worse. The industry that spawned the Eagle and Phenix Mill is long gone to Asia, and many of the fields that once produced cotton now grow pulpwood. Although Yankees have reoccupied northern Virginia, southern Florida, and large parts of Atlanta, the bitterness that I knew along the north Georgia home of my grandparents has dissipated, and my Negro friends are now colleagues. The world has changed for Southerners, both black and white.

But there are still places where, on country roads in the heat of summer, perspiration will streak the red dust on your forehead; where black water bayous meander among magnolias and live oaks; and where the long leaf stand tall and straight above a floor of palmetto or wire grass. That South is still there, and those of us who love her will be refreshed and reminded of this by these drawings.

catalogue of works

Georgia Pelican, circa 1791–1809
Watercolor on paper, 11 x 8½ inches
Inscribed lower center: *153*

JOHN ABBOT (1751–1840)

One of the earliest and most prolific artist-naturalists to work in America, John Abbot was born in London in 1751, the son of an attorney. Abbot wrote that he acquired "an early taste for drawing, which might be much increased by my father having a large & valuable collection of prints, of some of the best Masters, he had also many good paintings."[1] The young artist also received private instruction from the engraver and drawing master Jacob Bonneau. By age sixteen, Abbot had taught himself watercolors and began making scientific illustrations of insects in that medium. He was briefly apprenticed to his father as a law clerk, but his abiding passion was the study and practice of natural history. Abbot became an adept "Flycatcher" and illustrator, exhibiting two butterfly watercolors in the Society of Artists of Great Britain in 1770.[2]

Through Bonneau and others, Abbot became engaged with a prominent circle of natural scientists and collectors in London and, by 1773, had emigrated to America, armed with commissions from the Royal Society and private patrons. He settled in Jamestown, Virginia and spent two years exploring the area.

Seeking to avoid pre-Revolutionary activity in Virginia, Abbot left for Georgia in late 1775, settling northwest of Savannah in St. George Parish (later Burke County) the following year. He remained active in Georgia over the next five decades, avidly collecting and documenting natural history specimens, producing watercolors, and shipping his work to leading scientists, collectors, and publishers in the United States and Europe. He married, and the couple had a son in 1779. While best known for insect studies, he expanded his activity to include ornithological and botanical subjects.

Abbot produced hundreds of watercolors of birds rendered in a traditional, realistic style with delicate coloring. Characteristically, he portrayed the bird in a flattened, but revealing, profile view, on an abstracted fragment of natural habitat, such as the rock and marsh grass of this example. His earliest dated group of bird watercolors consisted of one hundred works done in 1791, which he shipped to John Francillon, his London agent and fellow naturalist. Francillon eventually sold them to Chetham's Library in Manchester, England. The library commissioned additional watercolors, which Abbot sent in two groups in 1805 and 1809. *Georgia Pelican* comes from this important historical collection.

Throughout his long and productive career, Abbot produced and shared his work with the most eminent scientists and publishers of his day, including Thomas Martyn, Dru Drury, and John Latham in London, who incorporated Abbot's ornithological notes in his ten-volume *General History of Birds* (1821-1824). In America, he accompanied the famous Philadelphia-based ornithologist Alexander Wilson during his 1809 visit through Georgia. Some of Abbot's discoveries and descriptions were included in Wilson's pioneering volume, *American Ornithology* (1808-1813). Abbot likewise associated with important Southern-based naturalists like Augustus Oemler of Savannah, and Charleston's John Bachman and Stephen Elliott, contributing to Elliott's *Sketch of the Botany of South-Carolina and Georgia* (1816-1824). He maintained an active career in Georgia until late in life.

RS

In May 1847, Massachusetts Senator Daniel Webster, a member of the nineteenth century "Great Triumvirate" along with John C. Calhoun of South Carolina and Henry Clay of Kentucky, took an extended tour of the Southern states. His purpose was two-fold: to appraise his prospects of becoming the Whig Party presidential candidate in 1848 and to gauge public opinion regarding the Mexican War. He arrived in Columbia, South Carolina on May 12, 1847, departing five days later on May 17. During his visit, he toured the city sights; traveled to nearby Millwood Plantation, the home of Wade Hampton III; and went fishing with local dignitaries. On May 13, Webster delivered a speech at a meeting of the Clariosophic and Euphradian Societies of South Carolina College. Because the South Carolina Assembly was in session at the time, he had no opportunity to address the legislature. However, he did visit the Senate Chamber of the State House, where Edward John Arthur—likely a member of the host entourage—made this pen and pencil drawing of him.

Arthur was born in Lexington District, South Carolina in 1814. He entered the local bar in 1835 and practiced law for the remainder of his life. In 1850, Arthur was elected to the General Assembly from Richland District. He served in the state House of Representatives and Senate during and after the Civil War. From 1855 to 1857, Arthur was mayor of Columbia; following the war, he was named city surveyor and a trustee of South Carolina College. A leader in the temperance movement, he edited *The Temperance Advocate* and other related publications from 1840 to 1854.

Arthur was a strong supporter of secession; his brother, Benjamin Franklin Arthur, was secretary of the 1860 Secession Convention. In February 1865, as Columbia was about to fall to General William T. Sherman's Union forces, the Arthur brothers escaped from the city, carrying with them the records of the Secession Convention, thereby preserving them from destruction.

According to family history, Arthur was a skilled caricaturist and some of his likenesses of Union officers were published in Northern newspapers. General Sherman was believed to have taken great offense at Arthur's depiction of him and supposedly singled out the Arthur home for destruction in the fires that engulfed Columbia on February 17, 1865. Both Arthur's law office and home were destroyed in the blaze.

AM

Daniel Webster (1782–1852), 1847
Ink and pencil on paper, 9 x 7⅞ inches
Signed lower center: *Hon. Daniel Webster./drawn in the Senate Chambers/*
Columbia. S.C./By E.D. Arthur (illegible four letters at end of signature)
Collection of Mr. and Mrs. David P. Riggins

Tybee Island, Savannah, Georgia, 1949
Watercolor on paper, 21 x 14 inches
Signed lower center: *George Beattie jr '49*
Signed lower right: *GEORGE BEATTIE JR/1949*

George Beattie was born in Cleveland, Ohio and attended the Cleveland School of Art. Known for landscape, genre, and mural paintings, he was active within the state of Georgia. Also an art educator, Beattie exhibited at the Cress Gallery at the University of Tennessee, Chattanooga and at the Art Institute of Chicago. His work is represented in the collections of the Montclair Art Museum; High Museum of Art; Georgia Museum of Art; and Whitney Museum of American Art. A cycle of the artist's murals in the Federal Post Office of Macon, Georgia depicts regional history themes. In the vibrant manner of social realism of the 1930s and 1940s, Beattie depicted a woman in casual beach attire on the pier at Tybee Island, a resort community located close to Savannah. A skillful watercolorist, Beattie conveys the sea breeze gently blowing through the woman's sheer dress and the strong contrasts of reflected light and shadow typical of the coastal atmosphere.

VAL

Dog River, Alabama, 1930
Watercolor on paper, 14½ x 22½ inches
Signed lower left: *F.W. Benson/'30*

Raised in privileged circumstances in Salem, Massachusetts, Frank Benson began his formal training in 1880 at the School of the Museum of Fine Arts in Boston, honing his skills alongside Edmund Tarbell, who would become his lifelong colleague and friend. He continued his training in 1883 at the Académie Julien in Paris. While in Europe, Benson also painted at the art colony of Concarneau in Brittany and traveled with Tarbell through Germany, Italy, and England. On his return to America in 1885, he opened a studio in Salem and worked as a portrait painter. The following year, he began his influential career as a teacher, first at the Portland Society of Arts in Maine, and then at the Boston Museum School, where he and Tarbell taught jointly from 1889 until 1913. During their twenty-four year tenure, the two painters often exhibited together and were closely associated in the critical press as the leaders of the Boston school.

Benson's oil paintings of the 1890s, chiefly women in atmospheric interiors, reveal an interest in decorative design, especially evident in an 1896 mural cycle for the Library of Congress. In 1898, he became a founding member of the Ten American Painters and turned his attention to outdoor subjects. After 1901, when he purchased a summer home on the Maine island of North Haven, Benson developed a mature impressionist style, frequently depicting his wife and children in dazzling sunlight. The paintings of the female members of the family, often dressed in white and silhouetted against a summer landscape, were lauded as ideals of American womanhood.

In the mid-teens, Benson turned to sporting scenes, especially salmon fishing and duck hunting, painting them in oil and watercolor. After 1912, he also worked as a printmaker. Benson was one of the most exhibited and most honored painters of his generation, winning almost every significant award of the day in all the mediums in which he worked, a rare achievement for an artist.

In 1921, while preparing for his annual fishing trip to northern Canada, Benson packed a pad of watercolor paper and a tin of paints. Captivated by the immediacy of the medium, he recorded everything in sight—the salmon, fishermen, canoes, and campsite. Back in Salem, the watercolors continued. He painted flowers from the family garden, his daughters in sunlight, the woods, pond, and autumn colors.

Dog River, Alabama illustrates Benson's mastery of the medium, as well as the effective use of the white of the watercolor paper itself. The river—located off the Gulf of Mexico on Mobile Bay—was one of the artist's favorite fishing spots, and he painted the motif a number of times. Benson utilized a variety of effects when creating his works on paper. Sometimes he used the medium very precisely, as a form of colored drawing. On other occasions he worked in broad washes, letting intensely saturated pigments flow freely across the paper, as in this example, where his focus was on the light, hue, and atmosphere of the place, rather than its scenic value.

31

SANDOR BERNATH (1892–1984)

Best known for his watercolors of sailing yachts executed in a crisp Precisionist style, Sandor Bernath was born in Hungary and lived in Budapest before immigrating to New York. By 1918, he had begun to establish himself in the art life of the city. Although slightly younger than Edward Hopper and the Precisionist painters Charles Sheeler and Charles Demuth, Bernath adopted both their aesthetic and subject matter. He made his professional debut in 1922 with a solo show at Mrs. Malcolm's Gallery on East Sixty-fourth Street. The exhibition of nineteen watercolors included both New York and European subjects, indicating that Bernath had spent time abroad. In 1923, he turned his attention to seascapes of the New England coastline. During the twenties, he became a member of the New York Water Color Club, American Water Color Society, and Brooklyn Society of Modern Artists, and exhibited at the Whitney Museum and Art Institute of Chicago. Like many of his peers, Bernath worked as a teacher and illustrator to support himself. In the late 1920s, he moved to Eastport, Maine, where he continued to live until at least 1945. According to one source, he spent the last years of his life in South America and died in Belize in 1984.

While Eastport remained his primary residence, Bernath visited and painted in a number of American art colonies —including Provincetown on Cape Cod—producing streetscapes and architectural views reminiscent of Hopper. In 1935, he traveled to Taos, New Mexico and painted the church at Rancho de Taos, as well as a pink adobe structure surrounded by desert blooms. Bernath visited Charleston in 1937. Like many artists, including Hopper, he was drawn to its rural cabins, moss-hung trees, historic churches, and Civil War monuments. Accordingly, he approached the subject of *The Battery* with a cool palette and smoothly delineated forms. Although the sky is restricted to a small area, it is full of weather. The dramatic background reveals Bernath's sensitivity to a particular place, season, and atmosphere.

NRS

The Battery, Charleston, South Carolina, 1937
Watercolor on paper, 9½ x 16½ inches
Signed lower right: *CHARLESTON S.C. Sandor Bernath—37*

Fishing, Folly Beach, Charleston, circa 1930
Ink and watercolor on paper, 11 x 14 inches
Inscribed vertically at lower right: 72

GEORGE BIDDLE (1885–1973)

George Biddle, well educated, deeply cultured, and widely traveled, led an eclectic and peripatetic life that encompassed a broad array of life experiences. He largely worked in a style of social realism, though his skills were multi-faceted as borne out in works in oil, watercolor, pen and ink, clay, print media, and murals.

Born to a prominent Philadelphia family, Biddle attended Groton Academy; Harvard University, graduating in 1908; and Harvard Law School. He passed the bar in 1911, but changed course that same year to pursue a career in art, enrolling at the Académie Julien in Paris. He continued his art education at the Pennsylvania Academy of the Fine Arts from 1912 through 1914. That year, he returned to Europe, studied in Munich and Rome, and spent two summers painting in France. In 1917, Biddle enlisted in the army, serving until 1919.

Biddle's varied travels and experiences greatly informed his art. In 1920, he went to Tahiti where he spent nearly two years in a Polynesian village. He lived in Europe for three more years, spending much of that time in Paris. There, he met Jules Pascin whose art and friendship would be an important source of inspiration. Biddle returned to the United States in 1927, establishing a permanent residence in Croton-on-Hudson, New York. His travel was unabated, however. In 1928, Biddle spent an extended period in Mexico with Diego Rivera, returning again in 1940 and producing a mural. He also spent another two years in Rome, in 1931-1932.

In May and June of 1930, Biddle visited Charleston, South Carolina at the invitation of George and Ira Gershwin. The composers wanted his involvement in designing sets for their opera, *Porgy and Bess*. Biddle produced an extraordinary compilation of images—many in watercolor and pen and ink—that capture the particular rhythm and ambiance of Charleston. Several of these sketches served as studies for larger paintings. He also became acquainted with the novelist, DuBose Heyward, whom he visited in nearby Folly Beach. Among the works he produced was *Fishing, Folly Beach, Charleston*, which conveys the artist's skillfully minimal use of line to render apt caricatures. Biddle used a shimmering transparent technique in paintings and drawings, perfecting a uniquely vibrant and stylized approach to line, contour, and form that is a hybrid of modernism and social realism. Genre scenes of everyday life were a frequent subject during his Charleston residency.

Throughout the 1930s and 1940s, Biddle was instrumental in launching government art programs and participated in them himself, completing several murals. It was at the artist's urging that Franklin Delano Roosevelt (whom Biddle knew from Groton and Harvard) instituted the New Deal art programs, such as the Public Works of Art Project, crediting Biddle as its inspiration.

Biddle was an active teacher and writer. Beginning in 1936, he taught at the Colorado Springs Fine Arts Center for one year; Otis Art Institute in California (1941); in Saugatuck, Michigan (1947); and at the American Academy in Rome (1950-1951). The author of numerous publications, Biddle's autobiography, *An Artist's Story*, was released in 1939, followed by *The Yes and No of Contemporary Art* in 1957. He was an artist-correspondent for *Time* magazine in Tunisia and Sicily in 1943. A frequent exhibitor at many institutions over the course of his career, Biddle's work was featured in more than one hundred solo exhibitions.

Distinguished by his Southern heritage, Walter Biggs is considered one of the foremost American illustrators. He was born in Elliston, Virginia, where he spent his youth before moving to the city of Salem when he was ten. He attended Virginia Polytechnic Institute for one year, but left to study art in New York City. There, he enrolled at the Chase School (later known as the New York School of Art), studying with William Merritt Chase, Robert Henri, Luis Mora, Kenneth Hayes Miller, and Edward Penfield.

While a student, Biggs roomed with George Bellows and was also acquainted with Rockwell Kent and Guy Pène du Bois. He embraced a loose impressionistic technique and rich colors, but cited Henri as a key influence. Daunted by the challenge of earning a living as a painter, Biggs decided to pursue illustration as a career and soon met with success. His colorful illustrations appeared in such popular journals as *Harper's*, *Redbook*, *Scribner's*, *Good Housekeeping*, *The Ladies' Home Journal*, *McCall's*, *Cosmopolitan*, and *Vogue*.

Prodigious in his output, Biggs created numerous illustrations and other pieces for his own pleasure. He most often worked in watercolor and pursued colloquial Southern subjects, particularly street views, as in *Southern Scene*. Biggs' technical mastery and refined sense of narrative is clearly evident in this depiction of two African American gentlemen, decked out in fine attire, promenading through a park. The scene also reflects Biggs' particular penchant for social realism and for conveying a feeling of the moment, clear evidence of his study with Henri.

Biggs participated in several art organizations, including the American Water Color Society; Philadelphia Water Color Club; Allied Artists of America; Society of Illustrators; National Academy of Design; and Salmagundi Club. He taught at the Grand Central School of Art and Art Students League. The recipient of numerous awards for his work in watercolor and oil throughout his career, he was nominated to the Society of Illustrators Hall of Fame in 1963.

Biggs returned to Salem in the 1950s, where he lived out the remainder of his life; he maintained a studio in New York into the 1960s, however, and traveled there often. He left most of his work to the city of Salem and to Roanoke College, where he was artist-in-residence for many years.

VAL

Southern Scene
Watercolor on paper, 22 x 30 inches
Signed lower left: *WBiggs*

Hog Series XLIX: Tractor/Maria Teresa, 1990
Graphite, prismacolor, and watercolor on paper, 32 x 40 inches
Signed lower right: *©1990 Tarleton Blackwell*

Born and raised in Manning, South Carolina, Tarleton Blackwell received his bachelor's degree in art education from Benedict College in 1978. He was included in a contemporary Southern exhibition at New York's Metropolitan Museum of Art during his senior year, and it was on this visit that Blackwell was first inspired by the art of Velazquez. He continued studies at the University of South Carolina, earning master's degrees in art and fine art in 1983 and 1984, respectively.

Blackwell began the Hog Series in 1983 as a graduate art student. He was inspired by memories of growing up in the rural midlands of South Carolina, where his father, a Baptist minister, owned a pig farm. As a result, pork production was a major business that he knew intimately. In the 1990 drawing *Tractor/Maria Teresa*, Blackwell intermixes black and white sketches of feeding pigs, images of tractors, drawings of houses in a landscape, and a likeness of Maria Teresa, the daughter of Philip IV of Spain and Isabella of Bourbon. This portrayal, notable for the silver fans adorning the subject's wig, is taken directly from Velazquez's 1651-1654 oil portrait in the Metropolitan Museum collection. These elements—highly personal and emblematic—provide the allusive, layered, and subtle content that is characteristic of the artist's work. The storybook section and childlike drawings, for example, relate to Blackwell's experiences as an art teacher in South Carolina elementary schools. The fragmentation of imagery and montage scene, which blends the forms of a tractor with trees, reveal Blackwell's interest in Romare Bearden's use of expressive modernist forms and methods.

Although Blackwell has developed other thematic series in the course of his work, including the predatory Wolf and Fox, the Hog Series is predominant—the project with which he began his profession over twenty years ago and which he continues today. As he has explained: "The essence of the hog series can be related to the series of works Velazquez created depicting the jesters and dwarfs of King Philip IV's court. Velazquez portrayed these subjects as equals to their master. I have tried to portray hogs with dignity and respect, while at the same time revealing and sharing some of my past personal experiences."[1]

RS

RICHARD NORRIS BROOKE (1847–1920)

Born in Warrenton, Virginia, Richard Norris Brooke was educated at the Virginia Military Institute in Lexington, Virginia. Following studies with Edmund Bonsall and James Lambdin at the Pennsylvania Academy of the Fine Arts, where he also exhibited, Brooke taught at several schools, including the Virginia Military Institute (1871-1872). From 1873 until 1876, he served as U.S. consul at La Rochelle, France and subsequently studied under Benjamin Constant and Leon Bonnat in Paris. On his return to the United States, he settled in Washington, D.C. and painted two well received genre pictures of African American life, *The Pastoral Visit* (1880; Corcoran Gallery of Art, Washington, D.C.) and *Dog Swap* (1881; National Museum of American Art, Washington, D.C.).

Brooke's interest in black genre subjects was successful but short-lived. After 1881, he devoted himself almost entirely to landscape painting, forming the Washington landscape school with William Holmes, Edmund Messer, James Moser, Max Weyl, and others. Inspired by the French Barbizon masters and their Dutch and American followers (many of whom were represented in the Thomas E. Waggaman Collection begun by Brooke in 1882), the group recorded the fast-fading Arcadian beauties of the capital, especially around Rock Creek Park and along the Potomac.[1] In later years, Brooke shared studio space with Max Weyl in what were known as the "Barbizon Studios" near the White House, while living with his nephew in Warrenton.

In 1893, renowned genre painter and teacher Thomas Hovenden exhibited *Bringing Home the Bride* at the Chicago World's Columbian Exposition to great acclaim. That same year, perhaps in response to Hovenden's canvas and its widespread popularity, Brooke painted a large genre scene titled *The Home Bringing* (location unknown). In it, Brooke substituted a black cast of characters for the white subjects of Hovenden's work, seating them at a large wooden table, surrounded by family and friends. It was the artist's most ambitious African American picture since *Dog Swap* and, like the earlier work, was intended to show that blacks shared common experiences with whites, both individually and as family units. According to Brooke's notes, the piece was painted in Warrenton using local models. This drawing probably represents an early development of the composition. In the later sketch, the foreground figures have been removed, and the table has been brought up to the picture plane, so that the viewer is drawn into the scene.[2]

NRS

Study for *The Home Bringing* (also known as *The Wedding Breakfast*), 1893
Pencil on paper, 6⅞ x 10⅛ inches

Live Oak
Pastel on paper, 16 x 20 inches
Signed lower right: *Bruce*

PATRICK HENRY BRUCE (1881–1937)

The discovery of this early drawing by the artist Patrick Henry Bruce adds yet another illustration to the life and work of a man often ranked as one of the leading lights of modernism in American art. While his style may have been modern, his life was tinged with a tragic air. He was born at Tarover, the Gothic Revival Bruce mansion in Halifax County Virginia, scion of the colonial Bruces who traced their ancestry to the kings of Scotland and the Revolutionary War firebrand Patrick Henry. The family fell on hard times in the aftermath of the Civil War, and Bruce's childhood was spent in genteel poverty in Richmond. Both his parents, as well as two siblings, had died by the time he was eighteen. From that age, he was on his own, working as a clerk in a real estate office by day and pursuing his art studies in the evening.

Bruce's first teacher, Edward Virginius Valentine, was a distinguished sculptor, artist of the recumbent Lee Memorial at Washington and Lee University. His early studies were very academic in nature: life drawing classes with Valentine, along with more practical instruction in mechanical drawing and drafting at the Virginia Mechanics Institute. Valentine was a sophisticated and well connected artist, and Richmond, flush with tobacco prosperity, was not a provincial backwater. Bruce knew there was a larger world and "all he lived for was to study art in Paris."[1] He moved to Paris by way of New York, where he spent the year 1902-1903 studying with William Merritt Chase and Kenneth Hayes Miller, and made the acquaintance of Edward Hopper and Guy Pène du Bois.

Bruce was working in Paris in 1905, when he wrote to Henri that he longed for "really truthful painting," a comment which suggests a greater affinity for ongoing trends of Anglo-American realism and naturalism than for the form-shifting patterns of early cubism.[2] By 1906, he had met Gertrude and Leo Stein, and frequented the salons in their atelier. There, a panoply of artists on view stirred his imagination, and he became especially influenced by the planar field organization and color field dispatch of Cezanne. During this time, Bruce created still life and landscape watercolors with a distinctly Cezannesque flair; this is the style he presented in the famous New York Armory Show of 1913. After the First World War, he began to paint works in oil in a style William Agee has called "geometric architectural." Some scholars have seen a kinship between Bruce and the scynchromist style of Morgan Russell, while others note a connection to Fernand Leger's juxtaposition of flat massings of hard-edged form, both figurative and non-figurative.

In this example which precedes Bruce's modernist phase, a live oak dominates the planar field, dwarfing a small shack in the back. Like his fellow Virginian, the writer William Styron, Bruce may have had a sympathetic regard for "the landscape itself, sometimes unspectacular and ordinary (cornfields, pine woods, country stores) but more often possessing a sorrowing beauty—everywhere lovelier and more mellow and melancholy and fledged with green than the hard-clay country that dominates the higher elevations of the Upper South."[3] Melancholy would haunt Bruce's life, which he himself terminated in 1936 in New York.

Above left: *View of New Orleans*, circa 1852
Watercolor and gouache on paper, 5 x 7 ¾ inches
Inscribed lower center on border: *New Orleans.*

Above right: *The Bluff at Natchez, Mississippi River*, circa 1852
Watercolor and gouache on paper, 5 x 7 ⅞ inches
Inscribed lower center on border: *The Bluff at Natchez./ Mississippi River.*

Right: *Cincinnati on the Ohio River*, circa 1852
Watercolor and gouache on paper, 5 x 7 ⅞ inches
Inscribed lower center on border: *Cincinnati on the Ohio River.*

NICOLINO VICOMPTE CALYO (1799–1884)

Born in Naples, Nicolino Calyo was an accomplished American nineteenth century view painter who brought the discipline of his classical European training to vibrant portrayals of the American scene, like this view of *New Orleans*. He studied at the Naples Academy, where he learned Neoclassical, Italian, and Dutch landscape techniques and traditions. Calyo fled Italy in 1821, having participated in an unsuccessful rebellion against Ferdinand I (formerly IV), the Bourbon King of Naples. Over the next several years, he traveled, sketched, and painted in Europe.

Living in Malta from 1829 to 1832, Calyo taught drawing and then spent the following year in Granada, where his father held a position with the court of the Neapolitan-born Queen Christina. At the beginning of the Carlist War in 1833, Calyo left Spain for America, traveling first to the Canary and Cape Verde Islands, and then settling in Baltimore the following year. There, he held exhibitions of his large-scale European views before departing for Philadelphia and, ultimately, New York, which became his permanent home in 1835. Calyo arrived ready to produce views of the great fire of New York, which occurred on December 16-17, 1835, a pair of which were engraved as prints by William Bennett in 1836. Over the next several years, Calyo also created numerous characterizations of urban workers, vendors, and other street figures in the manner of Jacques Callot; a group of these were published in 1840 as the *Cries of New York*.

As an experienced landscape artist and traveler, Calyo made watercolor and gouache sketches on location, and these catalogued examples attest to his itinerancy on the Mississippi and Ohio Rivers. He traveled south to New Orleans in 1837 to exhibit his panorama of the New York fire and then returned in 1852 to display his diorama of the Mexican War (including wax figures). Around that time, he rendered this view of New Orleans, a valuable topographical document of the city at mid-nineteenth century. With precision and detail he portrays architecture, churches, and other identifiable landmarks, including the spires of St. Patrick's Roman Catholic, First Presbyterian, and Methodist Episcopal Churches on the left of the composition. In the center is the monumental dome of the St. Charles Hotel, while the smaller dome at the left represents the Odd Fellows Hall (built in 1851-1852), which helps to date the image to this time period. Calyo's composition is closely related to the popular aquatint engraving of New Orleans (1841) by William J. Bennett, from a sketch by another Italian scenic artist, Antoine Mondelli (1799- circa 1856).[1]

Because Calyo was such a talented figure painter (unlike many self-taught landscape artists of his time), the staffage figures on the river banks in the foreground give his work exceptional quality and a lively human presence—like the top-hatted gentlemen, one of whom gestures toward the steam- and sailboats. Other figures work or relax. Calyo portrays the light, color, and atmosphere of the view through his skilled use of watercolor and gouache.

Calyo continued to be active in scenic painting through the 1850s, along with two of his sons, John and Hannibal, and his son-in-law, Giuseppe Allegri. From known works, he appears to have done less painting during the succeeding decades before his death in 1884. Calyo remained cosmopolitan and international in perspective and politics during his entire lifetime.

GEORGE CATLIN (1796–1872)

The first major artist to offer a pictorial record of the Plains Indians in their own territories, George Catlin grew up in the Susquehanna Valley of New York and Pennsylvania. Following his first career as a lawyer, Catlin pursued a second as a self-taught portrait painter and miniaturist. He found his muse while on a trip to Philadelphia in 1828. Upon seeing a visiting delegation of Western Indians, Catlin thereafter turned his attention to Native American subjects. At that time, the fact of the American Indian's demise was commonly accepted, and Catlin, who longed for a subject worthy of "a whole life-time of enthusiasm" resolved to document their appearance and culture before either vanished under the tide of westward expansion.[1] He began his mission in 1830; by the decade's end, he had traveled thousands of miles and visited forty-eight tribes. From this odyssey, he assembled "Catlin's Indian Gallery," a collection of more than six hundred drawings and paintings, as well as thousands of costumes and artifacts. The collection toured American and European cities for twelve years and, in replica form, for another twenty. Convinced that his "Indian Gallery" was a national treasure, Catlin periodically offered it for sale to the United States government. Though he did not live to see his wish fulfilled, the original collection was given to the Smithsonian Institution seven years after his death in 1872.

In the late 1840s, Catlin began to produce sets of bound volumes of line drawings taken from earlier Indian subjects. These souvenir albums, which numbered about ten, were offered for sale to private collectors. Most are presently held in permanent library or museum collections. The drawings published here were part of one such album, which has been disassembled and offered for sale.

Each album was unique and included between 117 and 217 portraits. All are exquisitely drawn and reflect the artist's sympathetic regard for his subject. Each of the individuals portrayed is identified by tribe, native name, and transliterated name; a narrative description often accompanies the sketch. The subjects are presented as though they have just stepped up to the picture plane, pausing momentarily before the viewer. Some are shown in profile or three-quarter view, but many directly meet our gaze. All are dressed in native attire and carry objects that indicate their interests and taste. Commenting on similar works by Catlin in a lecture in 1889, Dr. Washington Matthews observed: "Whatever unfavorable criticism may be made of Catlin as a colorist, little disparagement can be made of his accuracy and spirit as a delineator. . . . His portraits were true enough to be recognized by and bring tears to the eyes of the children and the grandchildren of the departed heroes represented."[2]

NRS

Stu-cha-co-me-co (The Great King): Creek, 1852
Graphite on paper, 14 x 10½ inches
Inscribed by the artist on verso of an accompanying sheet: *77/Creek/Stu-cha-co-me-co (the great King) called:
Ben/ Perryman, one of the chiefs of the tribe, with his/Rifle in hand./A tribe of 15,000. partly civilized, & recently
removed from the State of Georgia, to the Arkansas, 700. miles/W. of the Mississippi.*

Tol-lee: Cherokee, 1852
Graphite on paper, 14 x 10½ inches
Inscribed by the artist on verso of an accompanying sheet: *184/Cherokee/Tol-lee (__) Chief of a Band, Civilized/
and half caste./A tribe of 20,000, chiefly civilized and/agricultural. All removed by President/Jackson, to the
Arkansas, 700. miles W. of the/Mississippi. They formerly lived in the State/of Georgia.*

View of Norfolk, Virginia, 1873
Gouache and pencil on paper, 3¾ x 10¼ inches
Inscribed lower right: *Norfolk*

Esteemed draftsman James Wells Champney was best known for his refined drawings and illustrations. Over the course of his varied career, he worked in an array of media, achieving particular recognition for his watercolors, pastels, and translations of works by the Old Masters. Born in Boston to the painter Benjamin Champney, he took art lessons at the Lowell Institute and apprenticed with the wood engraver Bricker & Russell in 1859. He served in the Civil War beginning in 1862, but following a bout with malaria, was discharged. He returned to Massachusetts to pursue professional art and also taught drawing at an exclusive female academy in Lexington.

As part of his education, Champney studied painting in Europe from 1866 to 1870, first in Paris and Antwerp; he returned to Europe in 1871, this time traveling in France and Germany. Arriving back in America in 1872, he embarked on a career as an illustrator and began a major commission for *Scribner's Magazine*. Working in conjunction with author Edward King on a series of articles entitled "The Great South," the assignment took Champney to every major city in the South, covering about twenty thousand miles and producing over five hundred sketches. This scene of Norfolk was a source for the wood engraving, *A Glimpse of Norfolk*, which accompanied King's 1874 article, "A Ramble in Virginia"[1] and also appeared in the series' expanded book form.[2] The graceful lines, fine detail, and scrupulous accuracy seen here are typical of Champney's black and white drawings. The expansive horizontality of the scene accentuates the sprawling harbor vista.

Married in 1873 to author Elizabeth Williams, Champney soon began contributing illustrations to his wife's children's books. The couple maintained a residence in New York City, periodically traveled to Europe, and summered in Deerfield, Massachusetts. In his work, Champney undertook a wide range of subjects, including landscapes, portraits, and travel sketches, as in *View of Norfolk*, most often working directly from the subject.

Champney was a frequent exhibitor and participant in major exhibitions, including the American Water Color Society; National Academy of Design; Pennsylvania Academy of the Fine Arts; Paris Salon; and Philadelphia Centennial. He was nominated an associate of the National Academy in 1882. In his later career, his focus shifted to portraiture, depicting society sitters and prominent individuals of the theater. He also produced mural decorations for the Hotel Manhattan in New York and was an amateur photographer. From 1872 to 1903, Champney served as a professor of art at Smith College, when he began working in pastel. From that time forward, he worked almost exclusively in this medium and came to be considered the best pastellist of his day. He died tragically in an elevator accident in New York City.

GEORGE HENRY CLEMENTS (1854–1935)

A watercolorist who specialized in coastal scenes, George Henry Clements grew up on his family's plantation near Opelousas, Louisiana. As a young man, Clements worked as a clerk for the New Orleans Cotton Exchange before turning to painting. He began his formal art training at the Union Art League in New York City in 1880 and by 1881 was living in Paris. He spent a year studying at the Académie Julien and another at the Académie Colarossi. Clements also painted in the French countryside, Switzerland, and Italy. He returned to America in 1887 and opened a studio in Boston. After the turn of the century, he settled in New York City, frequently visiting his native South to find landscape subjects in the Carolinas and the coastal regions of Louisiana, Mississippi, and Alabama.

Until about 1890, Clements' subjects were primarily portraits, narrative scenes, and figure paintings. During the following decade, he adopted an impressionist style and turned to marine and nautical views. Sailboats on Lake Pontchartrain and shrimp boats on the Mississippi were early motifs, and throughout his career he was drawn to sites from which he could admire boats—not only sailboats, but also luxury craft and industrial ships. Clements' 1901 visit to Charleston, South Carolina coincided with the opening of the Charleston Exposition, an event organized to stimulate trade through the city's harbor, where traffic had declined since the Civil War. While nothing is known about his stay, the visit is recorded in *Sailboats, Charleston*. Other compositions of the early 1900s offer more generalized titles and settings. Clements rarely dated his watercolors, and his style has no definitive chronology. His work is characterized by lively brushwork and a concern for atmospheric effects.

Though Clements also painted at Cape Cod and Santa Barbara, his reputation became inextricably linked to Southern subjects. He exhibited often and widely, and institutions such as the Cincinnati Museum of Art acquired his work.

NRS

Sailboats, Charleston, 1901
Watercolor on paper, 9½ x 13¼ inches
Signed upper right: *G. H. Clements/Charleston-1901-*
Collection of Mr. and Mrs. A. Dano Davis

A Cotton Plantation in South Carolina, 1891
Pen and ink with black and white wash on paper, 5¼ x 8¼ inches
Signed on verso: *reduciren auf 10 cm foj x 17 cmudka. A cotton-plantation in South Carolina*
Drawing by R. Cronau, made in 1891.
The Craft Collection, in conjunction with Dorothy Goldeen Fine Art Advisory

One of the most notable artist-authors of his time, Rudolf Cronau was born in Solingen, Prussia. From 1870 to 1871, he studied at the Düsseldorf Academy with Andreas Muller and Andreas Achenbach. He moved to Leipzig in 1877 and began working for *Das Illustrirte Zeitung*, a daily newspaper, and *Die Gartenlaube*. The latter, a weekly publication, dispatched Cronau to America in 1881 to produce topographical views and articles documenting city and rural life, industry, nature, and landmarks.

Cronau began this assignment in New York, Washington, and Baltimore before traveling to the Midwest along the Mississippi River. He spent time in Florida and Louisiana and, by 1882, was active throughout the West, including San Francisco, where he documented Chinese-American culture. From these excursions, Cronau produced numerous picturesque landscape and genre sketches of American scenery, life, and work. At Fort Randall in the Dakotas, he sketched Native American chiefs, including the first life portrait of the Sioux leader Sitting Bull.

Published in Leipzig in the 1880s and 1890s, Cronau's travel portfolios featured his descriptive essays accompanied by print illustrations made from the original drawings. During 1890 and 1891, the artist was again itinerant in the United States, Mexico, and South America, when he sketched this unidentified South Carolina cotton plantation. These travels culminated in the publication of his two-volume folio edition, *Amerika* (1892), commemorating the four hundredth anniversary of Columbus' discovery of the new world.

A Cotton Plantation in South Carolina is rendered in the detailed and precise topographical style that characterizes much of Cronau's work. He has created a scene that compresses various aspects of plantation life, focusing on workers in the field and at the cotton gin. Using a typical picturesque motif, he flanks the composition with the twisted, barren tree overhung with Spanish moss. In the background, a railroad passes on the land, as steamboats ply the river beyond. The plantation mansion and other buildings are situated on a rise in the landscape, under the lush shade of trees, a quiet, stately contrast to the industry of African Americans harvesting cotton in the sun. Drawing on his classical academic training, Cronau employs a defining pen line and washes to create interest in the plantings of cotton, figures, and other landscape elements.

Cronau served as a correspondent for the Cologne *Gazette* from 1893 to 1899. He settled in Phillips Manor (Tarrytown), New York and became an American citizen in 1900. During the early decades of the twentieth century, Cronau continued work as an independent author, producing the 1916 historical volume, *German Achievements in America*.

RS

Ezell's Brother, Greenwood, Mississippi, 1933
Watercolor on paper, 19¾ x 14 inches
Signed lower right: *Wm de L Dodge/1933*

Born in Bedford, Virginia, William de Leftwich Dodge spent his adolescent years in Europe, where his mother had moved in 1879 to study painting. Living abroad, he followed his mother's example, studying briefly in Munich and then in Paris, under Jean-Leon Gerome at the Ecole des Beaux-Arts from 1885 to 1889. This solid academic training resulted in Dodge's mastery of the techniques required for handling various media, as well as his ability to work on a large scale. Dodge achieved early success with several classically inspired works at the 1888 Salon and 1889 Exposition.

On his return from Europe, Dodge settled in New York City and established himself as a mural painter. Known primarily for his grand allegorical decorations, he fulfilled numerous commissions for public buildings and private residences, while also producing portraits and plein air landscapes. His interest in outdoor painting was advanced in 1898, when he spent the first of three consecutive summers at Giverny, France. Although his easel paintings are not as well known, he never abandoned this practice, composing luminous impressionist works in oil and watercolor throughout his career.

Though Dodge was not to make his mark as a society portraitist and had not yet received proper credit for his landscapes, by 1903 he was reported to be one of the country's most successful artists, artistically and financially. Soon afterwards, he designed and built an elaborate house and studio, called Villa Francesca, at Setauket, Long Island, settling there in 1906. In addition to oil and watercolor painting, Dodge experimented with illustration (for *Century* and the Paris-based *Figaro*); taught at the Art Students League and Cooper Union; and designed and successfully tested a model airplane/helicopter that flew twenty-five feet in the Tenth Street Studio Building. (One of the artist's model helicopters is owned by the Smithsonian Institution.) Dodge also maintained an active exhibition schedule, showing his work at the National Academy of Design, Pennsylvania Academy of the Fine Arts, and Art Institute of Chicago, as well as the American Art Galleries, Durand-Ruel Galleries, and Milch Galleries in New York.

Since his student days, Dodge had continually traveled to study and paint at scenic locales. Following a heart attack in 1928, he began to use watercolor with increasing frequency, ultimately attaining a brilliance that often rivals his work in oil. In the summer of 1930, he traveled with his family to Mexico, where he painted a series of watercolors of the Mayan ruins. It was on this trip that Dodge's daughter met Hunter Kimbrough, descended from an old Mississippi family, who would soon become her husband. Dodge visited the couple in Greenwood, Mississippi in 1933. During his stay, he painted several Southern subjects, including *Ezell's Brother*. Executed in a bluntly realistic style, Dodge focused on the subject's strong character, developing little more than his facial features, set against an almost abstract background.

NRS

WILLIAM H. DOUGAL (1822–1895)

William Dougal (née MacDougal) was best known as an engraver who enjoyed success on both the East and West Coasts, specifically in San Francisco and Washington, D.C. A native of New Haven, Connecticut, in 1859 he departed on a seven-month sailing journey from New York to San Francisco—around Cape Horn—with some colleagues who owned the *Brig Galindo*. On board, they traveled with supplies, which were sold for revenue, as well as passengers in pursuit of the California gold rush. While on this sea voyage, Dougal kept a journal and made numerous sketches.

Upon arriving in San Francisco, Dougal ran a grocery and livery store for one year and then returned to the East in 1850, settling in Washington, D.C. There, he was employed by the United States Treasury Department beginning in 1853. An accomplished engraver and watercolorist, he produced landscapes, portraits, and studies of animal life. The nation's capital provided Dougal with extensive subject matter which he translated into drawings, watercolors, oils, engravings, and etchings. He produced carefully recorded, detailed views of the developing city from various vantage points, as in these three historic views (see also pages 12-13). Dougal died in Washington, D.C.

VAL

Upper: *Washington, D.C. from Soldier's Home,* 1889
Watercolor on paper, 3½ x 14 inches
Inscribed on original cardboard mounting, now placed on reverse: *Washington. From Soldier's home./Dec. 13. 1889.*

Lower: *Washington, D.C. from Arlington Heights, Virginia,* 1889
Watercolor on paper, 6½ x 12 inches
Inscribed on original cardboard mounting, now placed on reverse: *Nov. 4. 1889 Washington. From Arlington Heights. Virginia*

Water Side—Iris Watch, 2004
Mixed media on paper, 51½ x 44 inches
Signed lower right: *W Dunlap*
Inscribed lower left: *Water Side—Iris Watch*

Born in Webster County, Mississippi, William Dunlap has spent the better part of his life in the South. After graduating from Mississippi College with a degree in art, he went on to receive a master of fine arts from the University of Mississippi in 1969. Having lived in several Southern locales outside his home state, Dunlap closely identifies with his regional roots: "The South is my legacy—the feeling for kinfolk, for storytelling, for customs and manners, juxtaposed with the polarities of social order and races—all set in that lush breathtaking countryside."[1]

The Southern countryside is a constant source of inspiration for Dunlap's art. His paintings are primarily devoted to landscape themes that are fused with varied imagery. Animals (particularly dogs and birds), flowers, and still-life elements are often superimposed in a way that suggests narrative, as in *Water Side—Iris Watch*, a work from 2004. While Dunlap's works appear to depict literal and familiar places, they are actually images synthesized in his mind's eye, composites drawn from his life experiences. Identifying this approach as "hypothetical realism," Dunlap noted in 1992 that "the places in my pictures are invented, an amalgam of all I've seen in art and the landscape. They aren't portraits of places . . . but they could be. I'm interested in that space . . . where memory and perception get all tangled up."[2]

As evidenced in this example, Dunlap often combines media, using aspects of painting, sculpture, and assemblage. With a carefully refined painting technique and rich palette, Dunlap juxtaposes the intricate botanical forms of purple irises against the dark foreground of a Lowcountry waterway with sun-streaked sky. The calm airless quality suggests an otherworldly atmosphere. Though his aesthetic is definitively modern, aspects of his approach hark back to historical references and traditions. Such a dialogue between the past and the present firmly places Dunlap in "the tradition of American landscape painters."[3]

Dunlap taught at Appalachian State University in North Carolina from 1970-1979; at Memphis State University in 1979; and at the University of Alabama-Birmingham in 1980. In 1980, he relocated his studio to McLean, Virginia; eight years later, he acquired a second studio in lower Manhattan. Dunlap maintained his New York space until 1990 and subsequently established a studio in Coral Gables, Florida. His work has been exhibited at numerous institutions, including the Gibbes Museum of Art, Corcoran Gallery of Art, Mint Museum of Art, Morris Museum of Art, Mississippi Museum of Art, and Ogden Museum of Southern Art.

VAL

FRANK F. ENGLISH (1854–1922)

Recognized as one of America's leading watercolorists during the early twentieth century, Frank English was born in Louisville, Kentucky and studied under Thomas Eakins and others at the Pennsylvania Academy of the Fine Arts. From 1881 until 1903, he exhibited at the Academy, as well as the Philadelphia Art Club and the American Art Society, while supporting himself as a commercial artist in Claymont, Delaware. In 1905, he traveled to Europe, visiting England and Holland. Five years later, he relocated to Point Pleasant in Bucks County, Pennsylvania, where he resided until his death.

While English also painted in oil and pastel, he is chiefly admired for his watercolors, which he highlighted with gouache and applied with a loose, delicate touch. He is best known for bucolic scenes of rural life—cider making, grazing cattle, harvesting chores, and horse-drawn carriages—images of an environment soon altered by expanding populations and technologies.

Most of English's landscapes record the countryside around his home in Bucks County or document his travels in Europe, particularly England. The moss-draped oak in this rural scene and the African American couple driving the carriage suggest that he made at least one trip to South Carolina, Georgia, or Florida. English rarely dated his pictures, and he reused descriptive titles like *Rural Landscape, Country Road,* and *Farm Scene*, making it difficult to identify exact locations. The same building (or one nearly like it) appears in the background of *Rural Life,* (circa 1900; present location unknown), along with the carriage and drivers.

NRS

Southern Scene, circa 1900
Watercolor and gouache on paper, 16½ x 22 inches
Signed lower right: *F.F. English*

Above left: *Portrait of a Seated Man*, 1853
Watercolor on paper, 9½ x 6½ inches
Signed center left: *JMF/Nov 18/53*

Above right: *Portrait of a Man*, 1851
Watercolor on paper, 9½ x 7 inches
Signed center left: *JMF/12 April 11/51*

John Mackie Falconer was born in Edinburgh, Scotland and immigrated to America in 1836. He settled in New York City and began work for a hardware company, which he came to control by 1874. Outside of this occupation, Falconer was a passionate amateur artist, widely recognized for etching and painting in watercolor and oil. Active in a number of arts organizations, he was acquainted with many of the noted artists of the day including Thomas Cole, Asher B. Durand, Jasper Cropsey, and William Sidney Mount, whose work, among others, he collected.

An early advocate of working in watercolor, Falconer participated in the New York Society for the Promotion of Painting in Water Colors (1850-1855) and was a founding member of the American Water Color Society. He was involved in several sketch clubs in New York. In 1848, he exhibited his first work, a watercolor, at the National Academy of Design and was elected an amateur honorary member in 1851.

In 1857, he moved to Brooklyn, where he was active in the Brooklyn Sketch Club and Brooklyn Art Association, and lent considerable support to the association's first exhibition. Falconer retired from business in 1880, sold his art and book collections, and moved to a smaller residence that had a studio where he continued to pursue his art. On painting trips, he traveled to Canada, the Midwest, and the South, and also recorded scenes around the New York area, favoring architectural subjects.

Portrait of a Seated Man and *Portrait of a Man* are likely the result of Falconer's involvement with the New York Society for the Promotion of Painting in Water Colors, which held informal sketching sessions with live models for "the study of local life character."[1] Falconer produced numerous studies of posed figures, most often male, executed in this fluid, naturalistic manner with skilled use of the medium's transparent nature over pencil marks. These studies are characterized by a lone figure, often seated on a modest wooden chair, with little suggestion of the background environment; they are routinely signed and dated in the manner of these two works.[2] Falconer's natural facility with the watercolor medium is evident in his convincing characterizations and assured handling of forms, light, shadow, proportion, and spatial relations.

VAL

Electric Cathedral, 2005
Ink wash on paper, 31¼ x 47¼ inches
Signed lower right: *Linda Fantuzzo 2005*

The art of Linda Fantuzzo, a New York native, is closley identified with Charleston, where she has lived for the past thirty years. An adventurous artist with a roving intellect, she undertakes varied subjects, approaches, and media in her work.

Fantuzzo trained at the Pennsylvania Academy of the Fine Arts from 1968 to 1971 and then again from 1972 to 1973, the interlude devoted to study in Europe and North Africa. Following her education, she settled in South Carolina in 1973. Though the Academy curriculum emphasized a traditional approach, Fantuzzo initially pursued non-objective subject matter with mixed media on a metal support, an aesthetic she subsequently explored for a number of years. She eventually returned to representational subject matter, first painting still lifes and then landscapes. This new focus on landscape subjects was inspired by a colleague, Manning Williams, who urged her to try working *en plein air*. Fantuzzo also produces interior views, which, along with landscapes, are sometimes combined with still life elements. Notably, the human figure is never represented, one of the few subjects the artist eschews.

While inspired by actual places, Fantuzzo's works offer the look or mood of a scene rather than literal representation. In this way, her style parallels that of the American nineteenth century landscape painter, George Inness, whose work and ideas she greatly admires. The most significant influence on Fantuzzo's intuitive and interpretive approach, however, is the American artist Edwin Dickinson. She works directly from subjects and also relies on photography to assist her as she reworks studies in the studio. Travel to Italy on several occasions furthered Fantuzzo's interest in traditional painting techniques, including glazing. In this example, she has employed a method of drybrush oil on paper which lends the image a hazy luminous quality.

Electric Cathedral was inspired by a power plant located on Charleston's east side. She was struck by the scene, photographing it in the fog one morning and returning later to sketch it on a clear day. As she revised and simplified her conception of the image, the structure that emerged on paper began to evoke a church with spires. The glowing light and vaporous fog contribute to the suggestion of the ethereal subject and atmosphere.

Open and experimental, Fantuzzo presently works in a style of painterly realism. Objects, architecture, and landscape are the subjects that stir her creativity. As she notes, "For me, painting has become a way to observe and to celebrate life. I find interest in painting a landscape as much as I do a still life. What remains constant in all that I do, is the attempt to render light and atmosphere. . . . The atmospheric conditions . . . [are] often the vehicle which conveys my response to this particular moment in time."[1]

JOHN KELLY FITZPATRICK (1888–1953)

Kelly Fitzpatrick was raised in comfortable surroundings in Wetumpka, Alabama and, except for study trips to Europe and military service in 1918, lived there all of his life. The grandson of a former governor of Alabama and son of a successful physician, Fitzpatrick was educated at Starke University School in Montgomery. He later studied journalism at the University of Alabama before resigning in 1910 to pursue his childhood dream of becoming an artist. Apart from a semester at the Art Institute of Chicago in 1912 and a few months at the Académie Julien in Paris in 1926, Fitzpatrick's style evolved informally through his independent studies and European travels. During the 1910s, he worked in an impressionist manner, but later incorporated the expressive brushwork and bright palette of post-impressionism. Like Van Gogh, whose style he admired and sometimes emulated, Fitzpatrick made his own frames, carving and painting them to complement his compositions. He painted rapidly, often completing a watercolor in three or four hours, and occasionally remarked that it took longer to complete a frame than a painting.[1]

Although the Alabama landscape was Fitzpatrick's primary subject, he also painted scenes of African American life, as well as several series of American Scene murals for Depression-era government relief programs. A powerful advocate for the state's artists, he was a co-founder of the Alabama Art League and taught at the Montgomery Museum Art School from its inception until his death. Having secured a reputation for his lively scenes of Southern life and culture, Fitzpatrick encouraged his students to portray Alabama with all its charm and beauty, using a "gaiety of color."[2] His most popular teaching method, painting the landscape *en plein air*, was adopted by the Dixie Art Colony, an art community established in 1933 and eventually housed at Lake Jordan, twenty miles north of Montgomery. The summer settlement, known as Poka Hutchi, flourished until 1948, attracting some of the South's leading artists, including Anne Goldthwaite and Lamar Dodd, during its heyday.

On the Lake, Alabama is a brilliant study of water, light, and atmosphere, all of which were preoccupations of Fitzpatrick's throughout his career. Commenting on his aim in these outdoor scenes, he wrote: "I guess I am an impressionist since my real joy in painting is to paint LIGHT and of all LIGHT, I like noon light best—the shadows are so reflective then and so full of color and LIFE."[3]

NRS

On The Lake, Alabama, 1945
Watercolor on paper, 15½ x 22½ inches
Signed lower right: *KELLY FITZPATRICK 1945*

Folly Beach, S.C., 1926
Watercolor on paper, 22 x 15 inches
Signed lower right: *FOLLY BEACH S.C./JAMES MONTGOMERY FLAGG/1 9 2 6*

Famed illustrator James Montgomery Flagg created one of the most iconic images in American culture: the World War I recruitment poster of Uncle Sam proclaiming "I Want You." Modeled on his own self-portrait, the poster was one of forty-six war-related posters he produced between 1917 and 1919.

Born in Pelham Manor, New York, Flagg showed an early gift for draftsmanship and became, by the age of fifteen, a contributing artist to national publications such as *Life* magazine. He studied at the Art Students League in New York City from 1894 to 1898 and became active in the Society of Illustrators and the Lotus Club. He then left for London, continued his education at the Herkomer School in Hertfordshire, and also visited Paris.

Upon his return to America, Flagg ranked among the foremost illustrators of the day, producing comic strips and illustrating books, magazines, and advertisements. His work appeared in such noted periodicals as *Collier's, McClure's, Cosmopolitan, Redbook, Leslie's Illustrated Weekly, Saturday Evening Post, Hearst's International,* and many others. In addition to his commercial success in graphic art, he was also a noted portrait painter and exhibited his work at the New York Watercolour Club, National Academy of Design in New York, and Paris Salon of 1900.

Though he is most recognized for illustration and caricature, Flagg was also proficient and worked in a variety of media and genres, including pure landscape. Evident in this watercolor landscape, *Folly Beach, S.C.,* is the artist's solid and unwavering technique. The lush coastal foliage in the view highlights his skill in rendering form with only the most minimal suggestion of details, producing a dense, richly-toned, and varied landscape scene.

A bon vivant, Flagg lived a hedonistic existence, pursuing pleasure and surrounding himself with beautiful women, sophisticated artists, and famous writers and entertainers. Though based in New York from 1904 on, he traveled frequently. Disciplined and prolific in his production, he worked consistently and enjoyed popular success. A detractor of modern art, Flagg died in relative obscurity in New York City, following years of failing eyesight and poor health.

VAL

CHARLES GRAHAM (1852–1911)

Born in Rock Island, Illinois, Charles Graham received no formal schooling as an artist. In 1873, he became a topographer for Northern Pacific Railroad for the survey of Montana and Idaho, a position which trained him in careful draftsmanship. He went on to paint theatrical scenery in New York and Chicago from 1874 to 1877, after which he gained an appointment as a staff artist at *Harper's Magazine*. A prolific illustrator, he remained at the journal until 1892. Graham was an inveterate traveler, visiting and painting various places. He was active in San Francisco between 1883 and 1896, where he was a member of the Bohemian Club and San Francisco Art Association. During this period, he also produced many scenes of Colorado, the Dakotas, and New Mexico for the Northern Pacific Railroad.

Graham visited New Orleans in 1884 and two years later made an extensive tour of the South with fellow artist Horace Bradley, a trip that resulted in illustrations for *Harper's*. Although he remained a contributor, Graham eventually left the publication to become a freelance artist, producing work for the *New York Herald, Chicago Tribune, Collier's*, and American Lithograph Company. Between 1879 and 1891, he exhibited watercolors with the American Water Color Society, and two years later was named an official artist of the 1893 World's Columbian Exposition in Chicago. After 1900, Graham dedicated himself to working in oil.

The Encounter presents a unique Southern genre scene with sentiment and precision. An African American man appears to have climbed a tree to obtain boughs at the request of two ladies. One woman casually sits on the ground at the base of the large tree trunk, while the other stands, reaching for a branch from the young man. The image is rendered with careful attention and much refined detail, evident in the representation of the women, lush foliage, Spanish moss, and surroundings that represent a Southern landscape. Executed in a nearly monochromatic palette of watercolor and ink, only the foreground and lower tree trunks in the distance are highlighted with a burnt sienna tone that enlivens the composition.

VAL

The Encounter, 1889
Ink and watercolor on paper, 13½ x 10½ inches
Signed lower left: *C Graham/89.*

Facades, Charleston, circa 1947
Casein on paper, 22 x 29¾ inches
Signed lower right: *HALSEY*
The Craft Collection, in conjunction with Dorothy Goldeen Fine Art Advisory

WILLIAM MELTON HALSEY (1915–1999)

As evidenced by a remarkable career that evolved over six decades, William Halsey was one of South Carolina's foremost twentieth century modernists, well known for his vibrant and expressive style in paintings, collages, and sculptures. Born and raised in Charleston, he received early instruction from Elizabeth O'Neill Verner and Edward I. R. Jennings. He spent two years at the University of South Carolina before meeting the Russian-born stage designer, Sergei Soudeikine, in 1935. Soudeikine, who was in Charleston working on the Metropolitan Opera's production of *Porgy and Bess*, urged Halsey to study at the School of the Museum of Fine Arts, Boston, where his fellow artist-emigré, Alexander Iacovleff, was director.

Halsey attended the Boston School from 1935 to 1939 and was awarded a Paige Fellowship upon graduation. Due to the outbreak of war in Europe, Halsey and his wife Corrie McCallum traveled to Mexico instead of Paris, as had been originally planned. This experience made him a regular traveler and influenced his art in both subtle and dramatic ways over the course of his career. The couple returned to Charleston in 1941, and then lived in Savannah from 1942 to 1945, where Halsey served as the director of the Telfair Academy art school. They resettled in Charleston in 1945.

Halsey built his artistic reputation in the 1940s and 1950s by exhibiting regionally and nationally. Created during this period, *Facades, Charleston* portrays a row of buildings rendered in flat, simplified geometric forms and lines with a pattern of rich, warm colors that reveals the architectural order and variety of the city. The image is a view in the neighborhood of Halsey's studio and is related to known examples such as the 1947 oil painting, *After Rain*.[1]

It was during these years, as well, that Halsey met New York gallery owner Bertha Schaefer, who urged him to move to the city to advance his art and career. Although he declined to relocate, she represented him in group and one-man exhibitions from 1948 to 1953. He received promising critical recognition in *Art News*, the *New York Times*, and other publications for this work.

In addition to cityscapes, Halsey also painted landscapes, still lifes, portraits, and figures in a graphic style, derived from a post-cubist tradition of exploring nature and abstraction in expressive color, lines, and forms. His art later developed a personal, painterly expressionism, often characterized by bold coloring, abstracted forms, and varied materials and motifs.

Halsey remained an eminent and influential art teacher in the Lowcountry, beginning with his early activity at Telfair Academy and continuing at the Gibbes from 1945 to 1953. He subsequently co-founded the Charleston Art School with McCallum and Willard Hirsch in 1953. From 1965 until his retirement in 1984, he taught at the College of Charleston and was instrumental in developing the studio art department there. The Halsey Gallery and Halsey Institute of Contemporary Art are named in his honor.

RS

CLINT HERRING (born 1962)

A representational watercolorist who works in a traditional style, Clint Herring paints scenes of contemporary life that are full of light, color, and sun. His aesthetic approach—informed by the examples of Edward Hopper and Andrew Wyeth—is based on an interest in geometric design, as well as his desire to capture the "unspoiled essence of the subject" and to communicate its "aura or mood to the viewer."[1] When no human element is present, Herring transfers these qualities to the architecture or to the landscape itself, using intense light to infuse subjective content.

Raised near Auburn, Alabama, Herring demonstrated an early talent for drawing and began painting in watercolor while still in high school. After studying art at Auburn University, he worked briefly as a landscape painter, before moving to the Florida Gulf Coast in 1986. There, inspired by the casual lifestyle and bright coastal light, he turned his attention to scenes of everyday life. Returning to Auburn in 1989, Herring took a job with a local design firm, spending evenings and weekends developing his own art. In the early 1990s, he began painting full time. In addition to commissioned works, he paints landscapes, streetscapes, and genre scenes inspired by his travels in the South and biennial treks to the Bahamas.

Captain's Quarters is one of a group of architectural subjects that record a 2005 trip to Charleston. Although he occasionally makes watercolor studies on-site, Herring usually works from photographic references. He typically makes a half-size study and then lightly draws the composition on larger paper, adding color and detail as he develops the scene.[2] Herring was attracted to the house because of its romantic qualities: the partially drawn shade, broken banister, and stained facade alluding to age-old artistic themes such as life's transience and the passage of time, and, on a more personal level, to the loneliness and solitude that is an inherent part of the creative process.

NRS

Captain's Quarters, 2005
Watercolor on paper, 22 x 30 inches
Signed lower left: *CLINT HERRING*
Collection of Rich and Gayle Silver, Dafuskie Island, South Carolina

Portrait of a Man, Jackson, Mississippi
Watercolor on paper, 6¾ x 5½ inches
Signed lower left: *Wm R Hollingsworth Jr.*

William R. Hollingsworth, Jr. was an artist whose identity and production was deeply connected to his home state of Mississippi and to picturing Southern life. Born in Jackson, he attended the University of Mississippi in 1928 and 1929. He then entered the art school of the Art Institute of Chicago, where he developed an interest in commercial art, illustration, and painting before graduating in 1934. Eager to remain in Chicago, he attempted to find work, but found the Depression economy left him without gainful employment. This turn of events forced Hollingsworth's return to Jackson; there, he was able to secure a salaried government job while pursuing his artistic endeavors in his free time.

By 1937, Hollingsworth began to achieve modest success, winning awards at the Mississippi State Fair and the Chicago Art Institute watercolor show, which further fueled his desire to be a professional artist. He left his office job in 1938 and devoted himself to painting and also writing on art. During the early 1940s, he won more awards and reached the creative apex in his career. Hollingsworth established an art department at Millsaps College, where he served as an instructor from 1941 to 1943. He became friends with local artist Karl Wolfe, from whom he received encouragement. Throughout his life, however, Hollingsworth was troubled by anxiety and depression, and eventually became demoralized by financial woes and the ailing health of his father with whom he lived. Prone to deep emotional responses—both highs and lows—the artist succumbed to despondency and took his own life in 1944 at the age of thirty-four.

Hollingsworth appears to have found the greatest joy in life from his work as an artist. While he was versatile in his output, his oeuvre was dominated by genre scenes of everyday life in the South, showing industrial as well as pastoral locales. Inclined toward African American subjects, he was progressive in discovering the rich source of imagery in segregated black society and culture. A particularly able draftsman who preferred working directly from his subject, Hollingsworth excelled at portraits and was a prolific sketcher of heads. He was also a gifted caricaturist, capturing the unique qualities in a likeness, as in *Portrait of a Man, Jackson, Mississippi*. This drawing reveals an undertone of sad beauty that characterizes most of Hollingsworth's art.

VAL

FRANZ HÖLZLHUBER (1820–1898)

A musician, illustrator, and watercolorist, Franz Hölzlhuber created a valuable artistic record of the American frontier in the years just prior to the Civil War. His works portray the character of life and labor in Canada, Minnesota, Wisconsin, and down the Mississippi River to Louisiana. Native American chieftains, railroad camps, and surveyor teams come alive in his paintings and sketches.

Born in Grundberg, Austria, Hölzlhuber immigrated to Milwaukee in 1856 to take a post as a music instructor and orchestra leader. From 1858 to 1860, he traveled north and south along the Mississippi River, creating watercolor sketches. During this time, *Harper's Magazine* and other periodicals hired him to provide illustrations for feature stories.

Hölzlhuber's sketchbooks and some larger watercolors reveal that he sought to create spontaneous accounts of activity and commerce, rather than highly composed, polished works of art. The artist's subjects include portraits of Sioux, Winnebago, and Chippewa leaders; scenes of Wisconsin logging camps; and views of African American slaves on rice, cotton, and sugar cane plantations in the South. *Loading Cotton on the Mississippi* portrays workers—perhaps crew members in red steamboat uniforms—moving bales of cotton from a storage barn on a high bluff to the riverboat in the foreground.

Anticipating his return to Europe, Hölzlhuber planned to execute a series of panoramic views of American frontier life for exhibition in Vienna. He filled his American sketchbooks with studies, from which he later made oil paintings and more finished watercolors, such as this example. In 1860, Hölzlhuber returned to his native country, where he worked as a librarian and museum curator until his death in 1898.

AM

Loading Cotton on the Mississippi, 1859
Watercolor on paper, 17¼ x 24¼ inches

Sunburst, circa 1955
Mixed media on paper, 24 x 19 inches
Signed lower right: *Marie Hull*

Although she was an accomplished landscape painter whose lyrical abstractions were widely admired during her lifetime, Marie Hull is best known for her portraits of Mississippi archetypes. Born in a small town near Jackson, Mississippi, Hull initially prepared for a career in music and taught piano after graduating from Belhaven College in 1909. Around this time, she began to paint and studied locally with Aileen Phillips before spending a year under Daniel Garber and Hugh Breckenridge at the Pennsylvania Academy of the Fine Arts. Returning to her native state in 1913, Hull joined the faculty at Hillman College and spent summer months attending workshops at the Colorado Springs Art Center with John Carlson and Robert Reid. In 1917, she married a local architect and began a lifelong career of teaching art in her Jackson studio, while continuing her own education. She took summer classes at the Art Students League in New York in 1922 and later completed her schooling as a member of George Elmer Brown's European study group in 1929.

Hull greatly admired Breckenridge's explorations of avant-garde strategies and credited him with stimulating her interest in modernist techniques and rich, bold color. She also assimilated the anatomically rigorous portrait style still favored by the Academy. During the 1920s, Hull painted landscapes and street scenes, some of them done in Europe and Mexico, where she and her husband traveled to study architecture. In the Depression-era 1930s, her attention turned from outdoor scenes to portraits of sharecroppers and African Americans. Hull subsequently progressed to abstractions, exploring various styles and mediums, including casein. By 1965, her work was often totally non-objective. She exhibited in Mississippi and in other regional and national shows, including the New York World's Fair and the Golden Gate Exhibition in San Francisco in 1939. Her work earned favorable reviews, numerous awards, and select prizes.

Sunburst was painted around 1955, when Hull was experimenting with the brilliant colors and the freewheeling calligraphy of abstract expressionism. Her abstractions were usually based on her own rapid studies—often made from the window of a speeding car or train during educational trips to New York, Chicago, or Philadelphia—so that only the essence of the scenery was recorded. She later developed this motif on several different canvases and watercolors into a series of thematically related studio compositions.

NRS

ALFRED HEBER HUTTY (1877–1954)

A central figure in the Charleston Renaissance, Alfred Hutty was born in Grand Haven, Michigan. He grew up in Kansas City and Leavenworth, Kansas, earning an art scholarship at the age of fifteen. He worked as a stained glass designer in Kansas City and St. Louis, where he attended the St. Louis School of Art. Inspired by the landscape art of Birge Harrison, Hutty determined to devote himself to painting and, in 1907, traveled to Woodstock, New York to study under Harrison. He established himself as a regular resident of the Art Students League summer art colony there. During this time, he continued design and production of stained glass for Tiffany Studios in New York City.

Hutty first visited Charleston in 1919, looking for a place to spend the winter, when he famously wired his wife, back in Woodstock: "Come quickly, have found heaven."[1] He returned to the city from 1920 to 1924 to teach at the school of the Gibbes Museum and thereafter divided his time seasonally between homes and studios in Charleston and Woodstock. In Charleston, he embraced the friendship, collaboration, and activities of local printmakers and other cultural leaders, such as John Bennett and DuBose Heyward, whose 1936 novel, *Lost Morning*, features an artist modeled after Hutty.[2] He began etching in Charleston in 1921 and was a founding member of the Etchers' Club in 1923. Hutty earned a national reputation as a printmaker in the 1920s and the following decades.

Hutty's work reveals his varied artistic roots in the social realism of the Midwest, as well as the picturesque landscape traditions of Woodstock and Charleston. He produced numerous street views of Charleston's high-style and vernacular architecture. These types combine dynamically in *Wash Day*, with its interlocking series of buildings, facades, rooftops, and stairways giving form, texture, line, and color to the composition. The figures, clothesline, and ramshackle outbuildings provide behind-the-scene genre elements to this vibrant watercolor.

RS

Wash Day, Charleston, S.C., circa 1920
Watercolor on paper, 17½ x 23⅜ inches
Signed lower right: *Alfred Hutty*

84

Harvest
Watercolor on paper, 12 x 9 inches

Margaret Moffett Law was born in Spartanburg, South Carolina to parents of prominent and wealthy Southern lineage. She graduated from Converse College in 1895 and then went on to advanced study at some of the nation's most respected art institutions. For her era, Law manifested an unusual degree of dedication and independence in pursuing her career.

Upon her graduation from Converse, Law continued her training at the Pennsylvania Academy of the Fine Arts, Cooper Art School, Art Students League, and New York School of Art, studying with leading teachers, including William Merritt Chase, F. Luis Mora, and Robert Henri. She also studied in Provincetown, Massachusetts with Charles Hawthorne; in Paris, with André Lhote, a progressive artist associated with cubism; with Lamar Dodd at the University of Georgia; and in Mexico City. Of the artists with whom she studied, Henri's impact was strongest, inspiring her to paint subjects from the world she knew. Henri preached to his students: "I am not interested in any one school or movement, nor do I care for art as art. I am interested in life . . . let your history be of your own time, of what you can get to know personally . . . within your own experience."[1] Law adopted this recommendation wholeheartedly, later crediting him as the most powerful influence on her art.[2]

After the conclusion of World War I, Law worked as an art teacher at Bryn Mawr College in Baltimore. She also continued to develop her own artistic style—a style that increasingly favored a modernist approach, more freely conceived and suggestive than her earlier efforts. Her work of the 1930s and 1940s, employing a vivid palette of color and bold, simplified forms, reflects her energetic assimilation of modernist principles.

In 1936, Margaret Law returned to Spartanburg, where she served as Superintendent of Art in the public school system and was instrumental in the founding of the Spartanburg County Museum of Art and the establishment of its permanent collection. Active in regional arts organizations, she enthusiastically exhibited her work, including at the Southern States Art League. She also mounted solo shows at the Montgomery Museum of Fine Arts and the Isaac Delgado Museum of Art.

Law is best known for her unsentimental depictions of African American subjects in rural and routine settings, usually executed in colorfully stylized watercolors and prints. In *Harvest*, a loosely composed watercolor, field workers are shown harvesting the crops. As she observed, "I put down what I see, wherever I am, and the result is a record of life in a small Southern town."[3] Though she studied with important and influential artists, Law developed her own individual style and became a chronicler of black experience in the South, attesting to her independent spirit and approach to life.

VAL

The art of Blanche Lazzell encompasses a broad spectrum of styles, influences, and media. Best known as a modernist, Lazzell is particularly recognized for her involvement with the Provincetown printers, as evidenced by her woodblock prints of abstracted shapes and vibrant color. She also painted, producing representational and cubist subjects, as well as abstractions.

Born near Maidsville, West Virginia, Lazzell studied art at West Virginia University in Morgantown, where she received a degree in art history in 1905. Following her graduation, she relocated to New York to pursue studies in fine arts. In 1908, she enrolled at the Art Students League and studied under impressionist William Merritt Chase and alongside Georgia O'Keeffe before departing for Europe. In Paris, she took classes at the Académies Julien and Moderne, studying with Charles Guerin and Charles Roesen in 1912 and 1913. Following this European sojourn, Lazzell returned to West Virginia and opened a small art school.

The years 1915 and 1916 marked a turning point in Lazzell's career, when she attended the Cape Cod School of Art in Provincetown, Massachusetts. Provincetown had become an art mecca, attracting artists from around the world. There, Lazzell learned from the influential teacher Charles Hawthorne and, more significantly, studied printmaking—a medium in which she would become prolific—with Oliver N. Chaffee. From that point forward, Lazzell divided her time between Morgantown and Provincetown, where she became an important member of the art community.

Lazzell returned to Paris in 1923 and remained there until 1925. Her art moved in a new direction then, influenced by her exposure to cubism and the works of Fernand Léger, André Lhote, and Albert Gleizes. Ultimately, Gleizes would have the greatest impact on her aesthetic as it developed toward cubist abstraction. In 1933 and 1934, Lazzell participated in the Works Progress Administration program. Later in the 1930s, she came under the tutelage of Provincetown instructor and abstract painter Hans Hoffmann, an association that would continue for more than ten years.

In 1940, she visited the art colony of St. Augustine, Florida and it was during this time that she produced the drawing of Fatio House in preparation for a print. The drawing reflects her careful skills as a draftsman and her spare modernist style. She rarely depicted figures, tending instead toward abstraction or cubistic interpretation of still lifes, landscapes, and architectural subjects. Fatio House, a former boarding house dating to 1798, is located at 20 Aviles Street in the historic district of St. Augustine. The house is now a museum, the center of a complex that includes the coquina stone house, a detached coquina kitchen, and a circa 1802 washhouse.

In her own work, Lazzell noted that she was inclined to work "for color values, form relationships, rhythm of movement, interplay of space, and sincere expression." She remained creative, productive, and artistically dynamic throughout her career, producing modernist landscapes, still lifes, rugs, and prints.

Fatio House, St. Augustine, 1940
Charcoal on paper, 14 x 12 inches
Signed lower center: *Fatio House, St. Augustine-Design for Color Print/Blanche Lazzell-1940*

Grazing, 1916
Watercolor on paper, 14 x 20 inches
Signed lower left: *Manigault 1916*

An enigmatic figure, Middleton Manigault was born in London, Ontario into a prominent and cultured family whose heritage can be traced to Charleston, South Carolina. Little is known of his early life. In 1905, he moved to New York to enroll in the New York School of Art, studying with Robert Henri and Kenneth Hayes Miller; his fellow students included George Bellows, Glenn O. Coleman, Guy Pène du Bois, and Edward Hopper. Initially interested in illustration, Manigault briefly turned to painting landscapes before launching an extended aesthetic exploration of modernist strategies.

In 1909, Manigault's work shifted abruptly from realism. Beginning that year, he experimented with widely varied approaches, and his work reveals the influences of symbolism, post-impressionism, expressionism, and cubism. His first solo exhibition was held in 1909 in New York at the Haas Galleries; additional shows there followed in 1910 and 1911. He traveled in 1912 to England and France, where he studied the Old Masters and also began painting landscapes with nudes and working in the medium of watercolor. Manigault participated in the 1910 Exhibition of Independent Artists and in the 1913 Armory Show. An acquaintance with Charles Daniel, proprietor of the Daniel Gallery, one of the notable venues for exhibiting American art in New York, led to representation by that gallery. Manigault would eventually have his work featured in three solo exhibitions at the Daniel Gallery, in 1914, 1915, and 1916. The shows elicited praise for the originality of his work and further established his reputation.

Grazing is executed in a more traditional vein than the artist's best known, highly decorative style, though he makes use of ornamental patterning that animates the interpretation of the landscape. A versatile technician in fine arts as well as crafts, he produced work in oil, watercolor, and ceramics, and also executed murals and interior design projects. In 1916, Manigault began to frequent locales in New England and in the Oneida community of New York. Three years later, he moved to Los Angeles and then, in 1921, to San Francisco, which effectively removed him from the hub of the New York art world. His late work was predominantly devoted to flower still lifes and some small landscapes.

Plagued by instability and depression, Manigault apparently destroyed many of his works and also undertook an extended fast that resulted in his premature death. A prolific and frequent exhibitor who received critical acclaim during a large part of his active career, Manigault was relegated to obscurity until a relatively recent rediscovery and reappraisal of his work.

VAL

CORRIE McCALLUM (born 1914)

Known principally as a modernist painter and printmaker, Corrie McCallum was born and raised in Sumter, South Carolina. She knew as a child that she wanted to be an artist and began formal studies at the University of South Carolina, where she received a certificate in Fine Arts in 1935. After a brief stint as a medical illustrator, she continued her education in 1937 at the Boston Museum School. In 1939, McCallum married fellow art student William Halsey and moved to Mexico. Two years later, the couple returned to his hometown of Charleston, where they established separate studios and embarked on independent careers.

During the 1940s and 1950s, McCallum raised her family, while devoting time to painting landscapes and streetscapes of Charleston. She also taught at the Gibbes Art Gallery, Telfair Academy, and Charleston Art School, which she and Halsey founded. McCallum later worked as an education curator at the Gibbes; it was during her tenure in this position that she developed an interest in printmaking. A 1968 grant from the Hughes Foundation enabled her to travel solo around the globe to find inspiration for her art. From 1971 to 1979, she taught painting, drawing, and printmaking at the College of Charleston.

Following her retirement from teaching, McCallum experimented with semi-abstract imagery, exploring various mediums and techniques. While these works signaled a new direction for the artist, the basic elements of nature, whether recognizable or not, remained the underlying theme of her art. McCallum maintained an active work and exhibition schedule through the 1990s and was the subject of retrospective exhibitions at the Gibbes Museum of Art in 1994 and at the Sumter Gallery of Art in 2004.

The impressionistic watercolor, *Ft. Sumter* was painted to accompany Halsey's 1961 *Ford Times* article, "The First Shot and the Longest Siege," an essay detailing Fort Sumter's pivotal role in the Civil War. Fort Sumter—named for General Thomas Sumter, a Revolutionary War hero and the namesake of McCallum's native city—became a national monument by act of Congress in 1948. The site was restored by the National Park Service for the Civil War Centennial, which was observed in the United States from April 1961 through May 1965.

McCallum's watercolor was taken from an engraving of the fort published in *Harper's Magazine* on January 26, 1861. Modeled closely on the original, the scene is described in soft pastel colors and includes sailboats, seagulls, and sunlight. Halsey contributed a watercolor to the article as well, an interior study of the fort, which details the intricate masonry of the walls and offers a striking contrast to his wife's sunlit exterior view.

NRS

Ft. Sumter, From a Contemporary Engraving, 1961
Watercolor and gouache on paper, 20½ x 26 inches
Signed lower center: *C. McCallum*
Inscribed on verso: *(FROM A CONTEMPORARY ENGRAVING)/PAINTING BY CORRIE McCALLUM*

Among the Trees, Edisto Island
Watercolor on paper, 13½ x 10⅛ inches
Signed lower right: *Faith Murray*

A native South Carolinian, Faith Cornish Murray spent the better part of her life painting in the Lowcountry. Born in Charleston, she attended Ashley Hall and graduated with an associate degree from Fairmount College in Monteagle, Tennessee. After college, Murray worked as a draftsman in Washington, D.C. during World War I and then attended Teachers' College at Columbia University in New York City in 1920 for two years, studying with the noted modernist Arthur Wesley Dow. Murray subsequently returned to Charleston, living there and on Edisto Island during her remaining years; she died in Greenville, South Carolina in 1984.

In her paintings, Murray often depicted the African Americans who populated Edisto Island, engaged in work and socializing, as in the watercolor *Among the Trees, Edisto Island*. The barrier island had been known for its exceptional long-staple cotton until the end of the Civil War. The onslaught of the boll weevil devastated the region's cotton industry, however, and Edisto residents turned to new crops, shrimping, and fishing. In recording these scenes, Murray distilled her realistic vision with an interpretive and more modernist approach, progressive tendencies she learned from studying with Dow. Her works—executed in oil, tempera, watercolor, and pastel—are characterized by strong clear color, bold design, and a fluid handling of the paint medium.

In 1936, Murray won the award for her outstanding entry to the South Carolina Art Association. She exhibited in the 1939 World's Fair and in local exhibitions in Augusta, Georgia in 1940; Columbia, South Carolina between 1935 and 1945; and at the Gibbes Art Gallery, Charleston in 1935, 1939-1940, and 1944-1945. Between 1930 and 1938, Murray taught classes through the Gibbes Art Gallery. Her work can be found in the collections of the South Carolina State Museum; Morris Museum, Augusta, Georgia; and Columbia Art Center in South Carolina.

VAL

IRENE HODES NEWMAN (1900–1982)

Irene Hodes Newman was born in Cameron, Missouri, but facts of her early life and training are not known. Her watercolors first appeared in exhibitions at the Society of Independent Artists in New York in 1930 and 1932, then in Baltimore Water Color Club member shows in 1939 and 1940. In New York, she was singled out in an *Art Digest* review of a 1940 watercolor exhibition at the Morton Gallery as "one of the newcomers who makes strongest bid for top honors in the group."[1]

Magnolia Street was exhibited in the 1941 annual watercolor exhibition of the Art Institute of Chicago and portrays a street vendor scene—most likely in New Orleans, where Newman worked. Like much of her art, it is painted in a modernist style, with vibrant, saturated colors and expressive brushwork. She creates a dynamic composition with an angular perspective; the juxtaposed planes and edges of the sidewalk, building facades, and awning lend "completeness and a sharp, peppery flavor" to her art.[2]

Newman lived in New York, although she traveled to Southern locales to paint, including Savannah and nearby Georgia sea islands. She participated in exhibitions at the Metropolitan Museum of Art, Art Institute of Chicago, Pennsylvania Academy, Brooklyn Museum, Corcoran Gallery of Art, and other institutions during the 1940s and 1950s. From 1948 to 1955, Newman was represented by the Milch Gallery in New York.

Newman died in New York in 1982.[3] A group comprised of twenty-three watercolors and five oil paintings from the estate of the artist were sold by C. G. Sloan in 1997.[4]

RS

Magnolia Street
Watercolor on paper, 26 x 20½ inches
Signed lower right: *NEWMAN*

Cocktail Bar, New Orleans, circa 1935
Watercolor on paper, 14¾ x 21½ inches
Signed lower left: *Karl Oberteuffer*

The son of French artist Henriette Amiard and American painter George Oberteuffer, Karl Oberteuffer was born in Le Croisic, France and attended elementary school in Paris. At the age of ten, he moved with his family to the United States, settling in Chicago. In 1925, Oberteuffer enrolled at the school of the Art Institute of Chicago. While a student there, he received an honorable mention in 1927 and the S. S. Peabody Prize in 1928.

Following his graduation in 1928, Oberteuffer became an art instructor and taught at the Memphis Academy of Art in Tennessee during the 1930s, and then at the Vesper George School of Art in Boston during the 1940s and 1950s. A beneficiary of New Deal arts initiatives, he produced post office murals in MacKenzie, Tennessee in 1938 and in Falmouth, Massachusetts in 1943. Solo exhibitions soon followed at prestigious venues, including the Art Institute of Chicago; Corcoran Gallery of Art (1941); Whitney Museum of American Art; and Pennsylvania Academy of the Fine Arts. In addition to these successes, Oberteuffer was represented by two of the foremost New York galleries of American art, Milch and Macbeth galleries, where he also had solo shows.

Oberteuffer was primarily known for his exceptional work in watercolor that depicted scenes of France and Germany, and, in America, of New Orleans and New England, notably Gloucester, Massachusetts and Boothbay Harbor, Maine. His images resonate with a genuine feeling of the unique character of each locale. He worked from life and attempted to portray a particular moment in time. Over the years, his style evolved from an impressionist orientation concerned with light effects to a more modernist approach. Capturing the essence of the subject through direct observation, Oberteuffer's watercolors highlight the ambiance and picturesque aspects of a scene from unusual perspectives, as in the detail-filled *Cocktail Bar, New Orleans*, where the artist engages the viewer with the diners.

VAL

Do Unto Others, circa 1950
Watercolor on paper, 10½ x 13 inches
Signed lower left: *A. O. Petressen*

AUGUSTA DENK OELSCHIG (1918–2000)

Though she worked in New York and abroad, Augusta Oelschig is largely identified as an artist of the South. Born in Savannah, Georgia and having shown early artistic promise, she enrolled at Savannah's Armstrong College (now Armstrong Atlantic State University) in 1935, and also studied with a local impressionist painter, Emma Wilkins. She transferred to the University of Georgia in Athens in 1937, where she studied with Lamar Dodd, before graduating in 1939. Oelschig continued her training at Henry Lee McFee's art school in Savannah, exploring still life and figurative subjects. When McFee left the area in late 1939, Oelschig took over his riverfront studio. It was about this time that she became acquainted with the prominent artist, Alexander Brook, who resided in Savannah intermittently between 1938 and 1947. Brook was to be an important influence on her work in terms of themes and styles. He also recommended her for a wartime teaching position at Alabama Polytechnic University (now Auburn University), which she held from 1941 to 1943. Oelschig gained recognition with her first solo exhibition at the Telfair Museum of Art in 1941.

Oelschig married James Petressen in 1947 and began using her married name professionally. The newlyweds spent an extended period in Mexico during their first year of marriage. There, she continued her studies and came under the spell of the famed mural painters, David Sisqueiros, Diego Rivera, and, most importantly, Jose Clemente Orozco, whom she was able to observe at work.

The Mexican muralists inspired Oelschig to initiate an ambitious mural project upon her return to Savannah in 1948. In seeking to depict the recent history of Georgia for a new Savannah high school, the artist proposed imagery that highlighted the civil rights struggle in the segregated South (including depictions of the Ku Klux Klan) and implied criticism of recent government stewardship. Her proposal was predictably rejected for its controversial interpretation. However, this event galvanized her personal ideology and inspired her to produce a number of related works. *Do Unto Others* reflects both Oelschig's expressive style and social consciousness. Grim in its confrontation with a dark reality, the scene suggests hooded Klansman as apparitions surrounding a tangled mass of lynched bodies. Like many of her works on paper, the work is characterized by a strong sense of narrative and draws attention to the plight of African Americans.

The artist moved to New York in 1948, where she remained for the next fourteen years. Though abstract expressionism was the prevailing trend, Oelschig continued to pursue subjects oriented toward social realism. In New York, she exhibited her work at the noted Ferargil Gallery and also at ACA Galleries. Her marriage ended in 1962, prompting her return to Savannah, where she sought a new direction for her work and taught art privately.

The major triumph of Oelschig's later years was the completion of a major mural project to honor the nation's bicentennial for the Home Federal Savings and Loan Bank in Savannah. Executed over the course of three years, from 1973 to 1975, the mural cycle, featuring forty-four scenes of historic Savannah, has since been relocated to the Savannah Area Chamber of Commerce building. Oelschig exhibited both social realism and still life subjects at various institutions throughout the South.

VAL

The Siege of Petersburg, Encampment and Headquarters of the 1st Brigade Division of the 9th Corps, circa 1865
Oil on paper, 6½ x 10 inches
Inscribed on verso: *Hd quarters of 1st Brig., 1st Div., 9th Corps. Down to South Side Railway, upon which the 9th Corps was doing picket duty immediately subsequent to the abandonment of Petersburg by Genl. Lee and previous to the Grand Surrender. All in April 1865—This is a memory sketch made after my return home. Jas. Wm. P.*

JAMES WILLIAM PATTISON (1844–1915)

Artist, soldier, writer, critic, and educator James William Pattison led an eclectic life. Born in Boston, he studied art in New York with James McDougal Hart and R. Swain Gifford; in Düsseldorf with Albert Flamm; and in Paris with Luigi Chialiva. Following military service during the Civil War, he went on to enjoy a successful career as a painter of figure, landscape, genre, and animal subjects, working and exhibiting both at home and abroad.

At the age on nineteen, Pattison was recruited to serve in Company G of the 57th Regiment of Massachusetts Volunteers, a squadron deployed to the Battle of Petersburg, Virginia. This siege, which extended from June 15, 1864 to April 2, 1865, pitted Union forces against well armed Confederate soldiers protecting Richmond in General Lee's last grand offensive. Lee's defeat in Petersburg led to the fall of the Confederate capital and the subsequent end of the war just a week later. As represented in this image, Pattison was serving on a routine nighttime security detail of the headquarters, which is seen here illuminated by fire. This oil sketch, executed from memory after the artist had returned home, is an exceptional record of a Union battle position.

In 1876, Pattison married Helen Searle, an artist in her own right, and moved to the town of Ecouen outside of Paris, where he remained for six years. Between 1879 and 1881, he exhibited scenes of Ecouen at the Paris Salon. He returned to America, settling in Jacksonville, Illinois, in 1884 and served as director of the School of Fine Arts there until 1896.

Pattison was an assiduous exhibitor even while living abroad. He entered paintings in annuals at the National Academy of Design; Pennsylvania Academy of the Fine Arts; Art Institute of Chicago; American Water Color Society; Brooklyn Art Association; and Boston Art Club. He also had work on view at Chicago's 1893 Columbian Exposition and the 1904 St. Louis Exposition, as well as in numerous commercial art galleries.

Pattison served as a faculty lecturer of the collection of the Art Institute of Chicago after 1896 and was an editor of the *Fine Arts Journal*. He was affiliated with the Park Ridge Art Colony, which was founded in the north Chicago suburb by Dulah Marie Evans and her husband Albert Krehbiel, and was comprised of faculty of the Art Institute of Chicago. The organization, whose mission was art education, was active between 1910 and 1915. Pattison was a prolific writer and critic, authoring essays on Robert Henri, Leon Dabo, Albert Blakelock, George Hitchcock, and George Inness, among others.

Following the 1904 death of his first wife, in 1905 Pattison married Hortense Roberts of Asheville, North Carolina, and they made their home there. He belonged to the Chicago Society of Artists; National Arts Club, New York; and the Palette and Chisel Club. Examples of Pattison's work can be found in the collections of the High Museum of Art, Atlanta, and the Union League Club of Chicago. He died in Asheville.

VAL

HOBSON PITTMAN (1899–1972)

Though Hobson Pittman spent the greater part of his life in Pennsylvania, his art is significantly informed by his Southern roots, particularly as seen in the dreamy, atmospheric landscapes he produced, such as *Moonlit Gardens—Cypress Gardens Near Charleston*. His oeuvre is comprised of varied subject matter that includes pure landscape compositions; spare still lifes; empty rooms or scenes portraying a languid, solitary female figure turned away; and interiors that include open doors, empty chairs, and windows. Through the use of these formal devices, Pittman's compositions often evoke isolation and nostalgia. This wistfulness can be attributed in large part to the artist's abiding affection for the Lowcountry and the South.

Born in Tarboro, North Carolina, Pittman began instruction in art as a child. He settled near Philadelphia at the age of eighteen and later attended Pennsylvania State College and the Carnegie Institute of Technology, as well as Columbia University in New York. He served as director of art at the Friends' Central Country Day School in Overbrook, Pennsylvania from 1931 to 1957, and subsequently taught at various other institutions including Penn State, the Philadelphia Museum of Art School, and Pennsylvania Academy of the Fine Arts from 1949 until his death.

In addition to a distinguished career as an art educator, Pittman was prolific and extremely active in showing his work. He first gained critical recognition in the 1930s while participating in regular exhibitions and annuals, ultimately garnering many prestigious awards. His work is included in many prominent museum collections, such as the Philadelphia Museum of Art; North Carolina Museum of Art; Metropolitan Museum of Art; Whitney Museum; and Phillips Collection. Pittman also became associated with the Woodstock art colony in New York, beginning in 1920. He spent the next eleven summers in residence there, working in the community and associating with other noted artists such as Yasuo Kuniyoshi, John B. Flannagan, and Arnold Blanch.

In his landscape subjects, Pittman was inclined toward a heightened theatricality and romanticism; he often depicted nocturnal landscapes like *Moonlit Gardens*. In this work, he depicts the unique topography of the marshy Lowcountry. The thin trunks of cypress trees emerge from the swamp, while the spare upper limbs of the trees are dramatically poised against turbulent, moonlit skies.

VAL

Moonlit Gardens—Cypress Gardens Near Charleston, circa 1946
Pastel on paper, 18 x 24 inches
Signed upper left: *Hobson Pittman*

Accabee, Ashley River, South Carolina, 1852
Pencil on paper, 8½ x 5½ inches
Inscribed lower center: *Feb 24, 1852/Accabee/Ashley River S.C.*

THOMAS ADDISON RICHARDS (1820–1900)

Though born in London, T. Addison Richards is widely regarded as one of the most accomplished mid-nineteenth century American landscape painters of the South. The son of a Baptist minister, the artist and his family sailed for America in 1831 and settled in Hudson, New York before moving to Penfield, Georgia in 1838. Once there, Richards issued his first illustrated book of art instruction, *The American Artist*, in 1838. A year later, he began his career as an itinerant artist-author, combining his interests in art, travel, writing, and publishing. With his brother William, he produced *Georgia Illustrated* (1842), an early travel guide depicting cities, natural attractions, and landmarks around the state. The volume consisted of steel engravings made from Richards' original drawings, accompanied by narrative descriptions. By 1843, the Richards brothers moved to Charleston to continue production of their literary magazine, *Orion*. It was during this time that the artist first befriended the eminent Southern author and editor, William Gilmore Simms, whose Woodlands plantation he would later sketch.

Ambition led Richards to New York City in 1844, where he entered the National Academy of Design for two years of study, launching a career-long association with the institution. In 1846, he began exhibiting landscapes at the Academy's shows and, in 1852, was made a full academician. At that time, he was appointed corresponding secretary and served for forty years. Richards' paintings were also included in the annual lottery exhibitions of the American Art-Union from 1845 until 1852.

Like many of his fellow artists of the Hudson River School, Richards, while based in New York, traveled widely in the Northeast to sketch and paint rural views, cities, landmarks, and estates. His early, abiding connections to Georgia and South Carolina, however, made him one of the few antebellum landscape painters to return south to portray and promote the region in his paintings, print publications, and articles.

During an 1852 trip to Charleston, Richards rendered this drawing of a neoclassical edifice at Accabee Plantation, glimpsed between moss-draped trees. As with all of Richards' work, this elegant sketch is done in a picturesque, topographical style that was characteristic of English and American view traditions. Accabee Plantation was the eighteenth century family estate of Barnard Elliott. It was well known for its distinguished line of owners during the revolutionary period and as a place of refuge from the British. By the mid-nineteenth century, the plantation had passed out of family hands and was described as lying in ruins. Richards' view depicts the rear portico of the house and is one of three known sketches of the estate. Like many of his subjects, Accabee's rich and legendary history would have attracted Richards to visit and sketch the plantation. Simms' gothic narrative poem the "Cassique of Accabee" (New York, 1849) would likewise have contributed to the artist's interest in the place.

During the 1850s, Richards continued to publish illustrated guidebooks and cultural essays on landscapes, places, and people for *Harper's* and *Knickerbocker* magazines. His 1857 *Appletons' Illustrated Hand-Book of American Travel* was the earliest comprehensive guide of its time. Richards also devoted himself to teaching when he became the first director of the Cooper Union School of Design for Women in 1858. He served as an art professor at the University of the City of New York (now New York University) from 1869 to 1887.

Although born in Ohio, Paul Sawyier is widely known as the "Kentucky Impressionist." He became largely identified with his adopted state, where his genteel family settled in Frankfort in about 1870. Hailed as one of the most picturesque cities of the South, Frankfort was an important source of subject matter for Sawyier and served as the consistent and principal creative inspiration of his life.

Sawyier received his initial formal training at the Cincinnati Art Academy, studying with fellow Kentucky artist, Thomas Satterwhite Noble. In 1889, at Noble's urging, Sawyier left for New York City and undertook instruction at the Art Students League with William Merritt Chase. He returned to Cincinnati, working under Frank Duveneck during 1890 and 1891, an interlude which marked the completion of his formal study. Sawyier then moved back to Frankfort, where, with a colleague, he opened a commercial studio specializing in charcoal portraits. The artist was soon persuaded by his father to become a salesman for the family's Kentucky River Mills. Sawyier worked there only briefly before giving it up with disinterest. He remained in Frankfort, living in his family home and caring for his aging parents.

Following the death of his parents, Sawyier spent several years living on a houseboat, traveling the Kentucky River and painting the surroundings. In 1913, he left for New York and settled in Brooklyn. During this period, he began working in oil—a medium he came to prefer, though he never completely abandoned watercolor. He remained in the city for about two years before moving upstate to the Catskills region, first to Highmount and then to nearby picturesque Fleishmanns in 1916, where he remained until his death. Sawyier was prolific, regularly exhibiting his paintings, but he worked largely in isolation, apart from other artists or artist communities. His income from his artwork was very modest, and he lived in virtual poverty.

Sawyier worked in a modified impressionist style, adopting aspects that suited his vision. He did not always work from nature, often relying on photography, and continued to paint many scenes of Kentucky even after he moved to New York. Sawyier's work in watercolor is exceptional for its sureness, crisp technique, and atmospheric clarity, as seen in these two lyrical landscapes. His watercolors were generally produced in the studio, and he devised a method of working while keeping the paper wet. There is little discernable stylistic evolution to assist with Sawyier's chronology; additionally, he rarely ascribed dates or titles to works.

These two scenes with their poetic inscriptions derive from a poem by the once-popular New England poet and writer, Rose Terry Cooke (1827-1892). Cooke's romantic poem, "The Two Villages," about the villages of the living and dead, inspired Sawyier to create three separate sets of watercolor illustrations using scenes in and around Frankfort as models. It is believed that all three sets, the most elaborate of which is in the collection of the Kentucky Historical Society, date to circa 1900.[1]

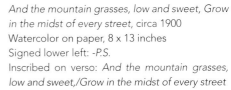

And the mountain grasses, low and sweet, Grow in the midst of every street, circa 1900
Watercolor on paper, 8 x 13 inches
Signed lower left: -P.S.
Inscribed on verso: *And the mountain grasses, low and sweet,/Grow in the midst of every street*

Longs to sleep in the forest wild, Wither hath vanished wife or child, circa 1900
Watercolor on paper, 8¼ x 13½ inches
Signed lower left: -Paul Sawyier-
Inscribed on verso: *Longs to sleep in the forest wild,/Wither hath vanished wife or child*

Centered around a road disappearing into the distance, *And the mountain grasses, low and sweet, Grow in the midst of every street* was inspired by lines from the end of the poem's first stanza. In the background, the recognizable church spire of the Frankfort skyline is visible. The second wooded scene, *Longs to sleep in the forest wild, Wither hath vanished wife or child*, portrays the cemetery where Sawyier was later buried and draws its title from the poem's last stanza. Sawyier's beloved Frankfort is discernible in the lower left of the composition.

VAL

Syncopation Number 1, circa 1939
Watercolor and gouache on paper, 9 x 6 inches

Best known for his emotionally charged portrayals of African American life in the rural South, Charles Shannon was born in Montgomery, Alabama and grew up in Ohio, Montgomery, and Atlanta. He attended Emory University, before spending four years at the Cleveland School of Art. In 1935, during his third year in school, Shannon returned to his native state and built a log cabin studio on his uncle's farm in the small community of Searcy, forty miles south of Montgomery. Though his plans to settle there permanently did not materialize, the summer's experience awakened his interest in Southern life and culture. "I began to feel," he later wrote, "what this country down here really meant to me. I worked with the Negroes in building my cabin . . . I went to their churches with them, to their dances and drank with them . . . I came to love this land—the plants and people that grew from it. My last year in Cleveland, filled with this newly realized beauty —I stayed out of school most of the year and painted Negroes and the Deep South from my imagination."[1]

After graduating from college, Shannon traveled to Mexico to study the techniques of the Mexican muralists. In 1936, he returned to Alabama and became an American Scene realist, creating genre paintings drawn from African American life in an expressionistic style of intense colors and elongated, rhythmic forms. Shannon's work from 1936 through 1939 brought extraordinary recognition to the young artist, including one-man shows at the Cleveland School of Art and at the Jacques Seligmann Gallery in New York City; favorable reviews in leading art magazines and newspapers; and a third prize at the Golden Gate Exposition in San Francisco for *The Lover* (Montgomery Museum of Art)—a painting of a distraught black man lying on the ground in a somber landscape. In the same period, Shannon won consecutive Rosenfeld fellowships to make a study of Southern types, the first of these scholarships to be awarded to a white Southern artist for work in the South.

In 1939, Shannon and a group of friends organized New South, a cooperative art center in Montgomery intended to facilitate and promote the work of local artists. Shannon taught a life drawing class there and encouraged the work of Bill Traylor, a former slave and naïve painter, whose work has since become famous. *Syncopation Number 1* and another variant version of the motif were likely painted at this time. Shannon was deeply attracted to the spiritual life of the African American community, and he went to their churches often, observing and sketching the congregants as they sang, worshipped, clapped, and praised. The dynamic, excited nature of the composition, as well as the bright colors and agitated brushwork, reflect his response to the shouts and rhythms of a typical church meeting.

NRS

Natural Bridge No. 1: View from the Arch of the Bridge Looking down the Creek, Rockbridge County, Virginia, circa 1820
Oil on paper on panel, 6¾ x 9¾ inches
Inscribed on verso: *No. 1*

JOSHUA SHAW (1777–1860)

This oil sketch of one of America's most famous early natural landmarks is part of the fascinating history and rediscovery of Joshua Shaw, an intrepid English-American artist, author, traveler, and inventor. It is one of a collection of eight oils that establish Shaw as an important precursor to Thomas Cole and the Hudson River School, and significantly broaden our understanding of early landscape art in the South.[1]

Born in rural Bellingborough, Lincolnshire, Shaw was orphaned at age seven and for years led a difficult existence with little formal education and various jobs. Early apprenticeships to a commercial painter helped him aquire technical skills and a reputation for artistic talent.[2] He went to London in 1802 and began exhibiting his work at the Royal Academy. Dissatisfied with his critical reception there, Shaw departed for Bath around 1804 or 1805. For the next seven years, he based himself at this fashionable resort city while traveling extensively through the countryside, painting portraits and landscapes. Refining his talents in the modish picturesque British landscape tradition, he achieved noteworthy early success.[3]

During his rising career, he had befriended Benjamin West, the celebrated Pennsylvania-born expatriate artist and director of London's Royal Academy. When Shaw decided to immigrate to America in 1817, West gave him letters of introduction. Thus Shaw arrived with considerable distinction and settled in the most culturally active city in America. In 1818, he began traveling to create sketches and narrative descriptions for his project, *Picturesque Views of American Scenery* (1819-1821), the earliest, most comprehensive aquatint portfolio of landscapes, rivers, and landmarks in the United States. Produced in collaboration with the master engraver John Hill, the prints reveal that Shaw's sketching tours took him throughout the eastern seaboard states from New York to Georgia, and possibly as far inland as the St. Anthony Falls on the Mississippi in Minnesota.[4]

Virginia's Natural Bridge, which Shaw calls "this great natural curiosity," is the subject of two compositions in the group of eight oils.[5] The view illustrated here is depicted from the top of the bridge, where the landscape expands in rolling hills, a golden pearlescent sky, and the winding stream below. A small figure crouches near the edge of the precipice, suggesting the daring height and grandeur of the view. In characteristic picturesque style, Shaw creates space and distance by the overlapping mountains and softening light and haze of aerial perspective. The foreground is framed on the right by shadowed areas of rock and ground, while rising into the sky are graceful, lacy trees—elements reminiscent of Claude Lorraine and his English followers.

For much of his adult life, Shaw pursued dual careers as an artist and an inventor of firearms components. Following his early sketching tours in America, he concentrated on scientific efforts in Philadelphia, and from 1822 to 1832 worked at the Frankford Arsenal. He was eventually awarded several patents from the federal government for his copper percussion cap and related parts in "the art of gunnery."[6]

In the 1830s and 1840s, Shaw resumed artistic activities, creating landscape paintings of British, American, classical, and historical themes, and exhibiting at the country's leading institutions. The artist moved to Bordentown, New Jersey in 1844, where he spent the last years of his life.

Bridge at Lavington Plantation, 1928
Watercolor on paper, 16½ x 21½ inches
Signed lower right: *Alice R. Huger Smith.*
Private collection

ALICE RAVENEL HUGER SMITH (1876–1958)

Alice Smith is one of the most celebrated and accomplished artists of the Charleston Renaissance, well known for lyrical, tonalist watercolors such as *Bridge at Lavington Plantation*. Born to a distinguished family in Charleston, she took early drawing and watercolor training at the Carolina Art Association, but was largely self-taught, developing her art through study, as well as association and friendship with visiting artists and friends, including Birge Harrison, Helen Hyde, and Bertha Jaques.

In 1914, Smith contributed drawings for the book *A Woman Rice Planter* by Patience Pennington (Elizabeth Allston Pringle). One of the earliest historical preservationists, she also collaborated with her father, the historian D. E. H. Smith, providing architectural drawings for two important publications: *Twenty Drawings of the Pringle House* (1914 portfolio); and the book, *The Dwelling Houses of Charleston, South Carolina* (1917).

Smith experimented with wood-block printing in 1917, producing exquisite, original Japanese-influenced examples. She explored traditional Japanese printmaking, using actual woodblocks collected by her cousin Alston Motte Read.

By the 1920s, Smith began concentrating on landscape watercolors. She portrayed the creeks, marshes, and swamps of the Lowcountry in a fluid style, as exemplified by *Bridge at Lavington Plantation*, painted in glistening tones of aqua, blue, gray, and purple. She centers the composition on the delicate construction of the bridge with a lone white heron, contrasted to darker areas in trees and paths through water and woods. Like many of the plantations Smith visited and portrayed during this period of her career, she was connected to Lavington by family relationship. Located south of Charleston on the Ashepoo River, the estate was a private hunting preserve. She created several other views of Lavington in 1928 and 1929, as well as another two decades later in 1948.[1]

Smith made sketches from nature, but generally composed larger and more formal watercolors in the studio. Her study of Ernest Fenollosa's two-volume *Epochs of Chinese and Japanese Art* (1912) remained significant in her creation of watercolors. Smith particularly praised the eleventh century Chinese landscape master, Kakki—an artist renowned for his rendering of landscapes in mist and haze. She was also influenced by Birge Harrison's discipline of "memory sketches," whereby the artist intensively studied a landscape view or fragment, made sketches, and then later rendered a watercolor of the scene from memory.[2] These methods gave her the more poetic and imaginative vision that she often sought in her work. Numerous sketches and sketchbooks also attest to Smith's careful observation and recording of nature, through annotated pencil drawings and watercolor studies of flora and fauna: "I believed firmly in painting things that I really knew, and in studying them until I knew them still better."[3]

In 1936, Smith published thirty of her watercolors in *A Carolina Rice Plantation of the Fifties*, her famous, retrospective portrayal of nineteenth century rice cultivation. Although her creative production slowed in the late 1930s and 1940s due to family illness and the war, she remained active until late in life.

Best known for his detailed and realistic Civil War marine paintings, Xanthus Smith was born in Philadelphia, into a highly accomplished family of artists. He was the son of the successful theatrical and landscape painter, Russell Smith, and Mary Priscilla Wilson Smith, who specialized in still life and floral genres. Both parents gave Xanthus his early training; he first accompanied his father on a sketching trip to New Hampshire at the tender age of nine.

From 1851 to 1853, the family (including Xanthus's sister Mary, who was also an artist) traveled to Europe, where in the classical tradition of the Grand Tour, they studied, sketched, painted, and visited art collections, museums, and important sites. Beginning in the Russells' native Wales, the Smiths went to London before exploring France, Italy, Switzerland, Germany, and Holland. During their time in London, Xanthus studied at the Royal Academy.

In 1854, the Smiths moved to a country home called Edge Hill near Philadelphia; Xanthus sold house views of neighboring estates among his first paintings. He continued his formal training at the Pennsylvania Academy of the Fine Arts from 1856 to 1858 and studied at the University of Pennsylvania medical school during that time as well.

In November 1862, he enlisted in the Union Navy and served as a captain's clerk aboard the USS *Wabash*, the flagship of the blockading squadron at Charleston and Port Royal. Smith's talent for military draftsmanship was immediately recognized by his officers, and he was assigned to create sketches and small paintings of the *Wabash* and other vessels. Smith took an eleven-month leave in 1863 to assist Admiral Samuel DuPont in compiling a book on monitors. The following year, he returned to active service aboard the steamer, USS *Augusta*, which escorted coal ships and monitors from Hampton Roads, Virginia to Norfolk, Port Royal, and Pensacola. Again, Smith drew and painted a variety of ships—including blockade runners and ironclads—as well as the naval activity that he observed.

Scene on the Beaufort River (circa 1863-1864) was sketched during his time in the Lowcountry of South Carolina. The image is characteristic of Smith's precise, topographical style and features a picturesque, semi-tropical view of the lush river coast; small boats and a larger sailing vessel; an outbuilding; the main house in the distance; and small, anonymous figures along the shore. This sketch may relate to a later small oil canvas, listed in the artist's 1867 account book as "On Beaufort River. S.C." As was Smith's usual practice, he composed many studio landscape and marine paintings from the storehouse of drawings and sketches rendered during his military travel.

Upon discharge from the service, Smith returned to Philadelphia. He divided his time between the city, Edge Hill, and occasional travel in Pennsylvania and north

Scene on the Beaufort River, circa 1863-1864
Ink on paper, 6¾ x 9¾ inches
Signed lower left in reverse: *Xanthus Smith.*
Inscribed lower right in reverse: *Scene on Beaufort River S.C.*

to the Maine seacoast. During his career, he was admired for creating a wide range of landscapes—from naval subjects to pastoral river views such as this finely detailed sketch. He exhibited his paintings regularly in the Pennsylvania Academy annual shows and major urban expositions.

Smith was very active in the decades following the Civil War, producing realistic ship portraits and meticulously documented battle scenes, assisted by his wartime sketches as well as maps, photographs, and eyewitness accounts. Between 1866 and 1876, he painted fifteen large-scale paintings that he called the "Civil War Series," representing the major naval engagements of the war.

115

RS

Morning on a Southern Plantation, 1910
Watercolor on paper, 22 x 35 inches
Signed lower right: *A.BS/1910*

One of the best known illustrators of her generation, Alice Barber Stephens grew up in Philadelphia and received her initial art instruction at the Philadelphia School of Design for Women (now Moore College of Art). While still in her teens, she mastered the mechanical processes involved in printing and began supporting herself by selling wood engravings to *Scribner's Magazine* and other periodicals. Although encouraged by her parents to become a full-time engraver, Stephens "wanted to work in color."[1] In 1876, she transferred to the Pennsylvania Academy of the Fine Arts and entered the classroom of Thomas Eakins, who was then beginning his controversial first year at the school. Under his tutelage, she turned to illustration, and her works in charcoal, oil, watercolor, and other media became regular features in *Century, Cosmopolitan, Frank Leslie's Weekly*, and the Harper publications. Remarking on Eakins' strong influence, Gordon Hendricks observed years later that some of Stephens' work "is scarcely distinguishable from that of Eakins."[2]

Stephens' painting, *Female Life Class* (1879; Pennsylvania Academy of the Fine Arts), was one of the earliest portrayals of women artists working from the nude. Commissioned by the Academy, *Female Life Class* brought positive attention to both the artist and the institution when it was reproduced in *Scribner's* in 1879. In the late 1880s, Stephens studied briefly at the Académie Julien in Paris and sketched in the Italian countryside. During her stay, she adopted a lighter palette and a softer, more impressionist style. She painted several richly colored landscapes of Italy and exhibited at the Paris Salon. On her return to Philadelphia, she married Charles Stephens, an instructor at the Academy, and began a successful career as a book illustrator. In addition to creating the illustrations for works by Louisa May Alcott, Bret Harte, and Arthur Conan Doyle, Stephens provided the images for a special edition of Nathaniel Hawthorne's *The Marble Faun*, a favorite travel guide to Rome for Victorian tourists. These were considered the finest book illustrations she ever produced, and the original paintings won a bronze medal at the 1900 Paris Exposition Universelle.

A burgeoning interest in architecture is revealed in Stephens' works of the early twentieth century, such as *Morning on a Southern Plantation*, painted in 1910. By that year, the family had moved to Rose Valley, an Arts and Crafts community within commuting distance of Philadelphia. The move was prompted by their friendship with the village's founder, the architect William Price, who converted a stone barn into a house and studios for them. There, in addition to her commercial work, Stephens painted figurative works and landscapes, often incorporating architectural motifs into her scenes.

NRS

Woodlands, 1943
Pastel on paper, 13¾ x 15½ inches
Signed lower left: *Stevens/'43*

Though born in the Midwest, Will Henry Stevens had a long association with the South. He came to New Orleans in 1921 and taught art at Sophie Newcomb College until he retired in 1948. From the 1920s on, while living in New Orleans during the academic year, he would spend summers teaching and working in North Carolina and Tennessee, where the richly verdant landscape and Appalachian Mountains were inspirations for his art. A man of far-reaching interests, his work drew upon various sources, including cubism, abstraction, and Oriental aesthetics.

Stevens studied at the Cincinnati Art Academy with Frank Duveneck from 1901-1904 and then went to work at Rookwood Pottery. In 1906, he enrolled at the Art Students League, where he undertook study with William Merritt Chase, Van Dearing Perrine, and Jonas Lie. A year later, he received his first New York solo show, held at the New Gallery. In 1912, he visited the Freer Gallery in Washington, D.C., where he was first exposed to Chinese Sung Dynasty paintings, which would become another important force in the development of his art and ideas.

An experimental artist, Stevens worked in varied media and incorporated ideas from a myriad of intellectual sources. Always innovative, he began pursuing non-objective themes in the 1930s, largely influenced by the work of Wassily Kandinsky. While actively experimenting with abstract compositions, he concurrently produced works in an essentially realist idiom, exhibiting his pieces in two different galleries, one for his nature paintings and the other for his non-objective work. Stevens' primary interest was in representing the fundamental spirit of his subject through color, form, and design, an approach which was foremost in guiding the direction of his production in either of his dual means of expression.

Stevens often evokes nature through the use of abstracted forms, as seen in *Woodlands* from 1943. While the composition references the concrete world with some identifiable forms, the overall composition is intuitive in its representation. Through his unique manner of applying pastel, Stevens attains a fluidity more typical of watercolor. His technical freedom also contributes to the poetic delicacy of his works, which sometimes feature a combination of media and techniques within one composition. The subject for *Woodlands* likely derives from the pastoral North Carolina landscape, though the composition evokes a universalized impression of the natural world.

Throughout his life, Stevens was an active exhibitor in gallery and museum exhibitions in the South and in the Midwest. Upon his retirement from Newcomb College in 1948, Stevens moved back to his hometown of Vevay, Indiana, where he unexpectedly died the following year from leukemia. Following his death, there had been flagging interest in his art until the late 1980s when an appreciation for modernism and its many proponents burgeoned.

Born in Rockport, Massachusetts, Lester Stevens received his early art training from Parker Perkins, a local marine painter. He later spent four years under Edmund Tarbell, Frank Benson, and Phillip Hale at the School of the Museum of Fine Arts in Boston, before serving in World War I. Returning to Rockport, which was then emerging as a popular art colony, Stevens went on to record the scenery there and at Cape Ann and Gloucester in a bold, impressionist-inspired manner. In 1921, together with fifty other artists, he founded the Rockport Art Association, primarily to exhibit the work of outstanding artists.

As the tourist population grew, Stevens abandoned Rockport in 1934, moving first to Springfield, Massachusetts and then in 1944 to Conway, where he remodeled an old farmhouse and continued to paint landscapes. He gave lessons in his Conway studio and conducted summer workshops in various cities, including Washington, D.C., Asheville, North Carolina, and Charleston, South Carolina. He also taught at Princeton University, Boston University, and the Springfield Art Museum. Stevens was a member of the National Academy of Design, American Water Color Society, and many other important arts organizations. He exhibited his work regularly throughout his career.

In 1939, Stevens staged a one-man show at the Mint Museum in Charlotte, North Carolina, where his work was well received. Southerners especially enjoyed his views of famous Southern cities, such as Charleston, where he often painted in the 1940s. Unlike most visiting artists who routinely sought out Charleston's historic buildings and gardens, Stevens was drawn to the city's residential neighborhoods, and he produced a number of street scenes, including *Charleston, South Carolina*. A superb craftsman and accomplished watercolorist, he painted rapidly and with assurance. And though he believed in painting "on the spot" and capturing fleeting transitory effects, he never lost sight of the fact that he was creating an artwork. He took time to find the best vantage point and rearranged details—such as the placement of doorways, windows, rooflines, and trees—to achieve the desired pictorial effect. Perhaps this is why Stevens would later conclude that "fine pictures are the result of fine minds."[1]

NRS

Charleston, South Carolina
Watercolor on paper, 20½ x 26 inches
Signed lower right: *W. LESTER STEVENS N.A.*

Sea Barns, circa 1962-1969
Mixed media on paper, 20½ x 26½ inches
Signed lower right: *Maltby Sykes*

A leader in the development of printmaking in the South, Maltby Sykes grew up in Birmingham, Alabama, where he learned to draw and paint as a youth. He had several important artistic mentors. The first was Wayman Adams, with whom he studied portraiture in 1934 in Elizabethtown, New York. During his stay in New York, Sykes met the lithographer George C. Miller and became his assistant. Upon Miller's recommendation, he went to Mexico in 1936 to work with Diego Rivera on a fresco project for the Hotel Reforma. He also trained in New York City at the Art Students League with John Sloan and in Paris with Fernand Leger, André Lhote, and the intaglio printmaker Stanley William Hayter. In 1941, Sykes returned to Alabama and joined the staff at Auburn University, where he taught painting and printmaking until his retirement in 1977. He was a frequent exhibitor, and institutions such as the Brooklyn Museum and Philadelphia Museum of Art acquired his prints.

Sykes' career spans more than thirty extremely prolific years, beginning with regionalist subjects in the style of Diego Rivera and moving through surrealism, lunar studies, cubist landscapes, and abstract motifs inspired by the Maine coastline. He began summering in Camden in 1962, returning there, and later to Booth Bay Harbor, for many years. As a result, Maine's harbors and hillsides became an important part of his artistic vocabulary. Although Sykes constantly pushed toward abstractions, nature as a source of inspiration is apparent in his work. The abstract patterns suggest such varied ideas as rooflines, the ramshackle construction of buildings along the docks, or the jagged rocks of the coastline. In *Sea Barns*, the architecture is reduced to simple geometric shapes and flat unbroken areas of color. The forms remain solid and sharply outlined, with their edges subtly aligned to unite the composition. Thin expressive lines define the brick, wood, and stone of the structures.

NRS

The Spiritual Society Dancing Scene, 1933
Watercolor on paper, 22 x 26 inches
Signed lower left: *Anna Heyward Taylor-1933*
Private Collection

ANNA HEYWARD TAYLOR (1879–1956)

Although she is best known for her brilliantly colored woodblock prints of flora and fauna, Anna Heyward Taylor produced and exhibited a variety of watercolors during her active career. This rural view of dancers and figures around a fire is distinctive in Taylor's oeuvre, not only for its array of figures, but also for its content, which focuses on Gullah spiritual rituals.

Born to a distinguished South Carolina family, Taylor was educated privately before graduating from the South Carolina College for Women in 1897. Determined to be an artist, Taylor settled in New York City between 1900 and 1901, and sought training with the acclaimed artist and teacher, William Merritt Chase, who became an important early mentor. She joined his first educational tours abroad to Holland and London in the summers of 1903 and 1904. Taylor returned to New York in 1906 to continue work with Chase and his associates, then traveled to Pennsylvania to study during the summer with William Lathrop, a leading member of the art colony in New Hope.

Returning to Columbia in 1906, Taylor embarked on a career that would combine teaching, study, and worldwide travel. Having already toured Europe extensively, Taylor made a lengthy trip to the Far East in 1914. While abroad, she befriended Helen Hyde, an American artist who had been living in Japan for years creating traditional woodblock prints. Back in the United States in 1915, Taylor spent the summer in Provincetown, Massachusetts, where she was influenced by that colony's innovative group of printmakers. During World War I, Taylor served with the American Red Cross in France and later joined scientific expeditions in British Guiana, assisting the noted ornithologist William Beebe as illustrator and botanist.

The decade following Taylor's 1920 return to America was a productive period, beginning with her exploration of exotic floral and plant designs in batiks. Along with watercolors and related prints, these became the first works she exhibited in 1921 at the Grace Horne Gallery in Boston; Brooklyn Botanic Garden and New York City's Museum of Natural History in 1922; and New York Society of Craftsmen in 1924. Taylor had a one-person show at the Milch Galleries in 1926, which received a favorable review in *Art News*. She participated in several prominent print and watercolor exhibitions in New York and Los Angeles in the late 1920s, before settling in Charleston around 1929.

Taylor quickly became a part of the flourishing regionalist art scene known as the Charleston Renaissance. Like other resident and visiting artists, she explored images of local nature and culture, filtering these themes through her interest in Japanese design and technique. For the next several decades, she focused on watercolors and block prints of Lowcountry subjects, including pastoral and urban landscapes, genre scenes, still lifes, and botanical studies.

Although her artistic production declined in the latter years of her life, Taylor continued to travel until her death in 1956, following her return from a Caribbean trip.

Oak Grove/Middleton
Pastel on silk, 25¾ x 30¾ inches
Signed lower right: *Elizabeth O'Neill Verner*
Bennie and Martha Team Collection, Greenville, South Carolina

ELIZABETH O'NEILL VERNER (1883–1979)

Born in Charleston, Elizabeth O'Neill Verner began drawing as a child. She studied locally with Alice Ravenel Huger Smith before spending two years under Thomas Anshutz's tutelage at the Pennsylvania Academy of the Finc Arts. Returning to her native city in 1903, she married E. Pettigrew Verner and raised two children. During this period, she studied informally, painting scenes of Charleston in her spare time and studying Japanese printing techniques with Alice Smith. In 1923, she took up etching. Two years later, she established her own studio and began a successful career as a printmaker and pastellist. Verner was a frequent exhibitor, and her work was acquired by such notable institutions as the Metropolitan Museum of Art, Museum of Fine Arts, Boston, and others.

The 1930s marked the high point of Verner's career as an etcher and the onset of her interest in pastel. She began experimenting with the medium in 1934, after seeing an exhibition of floral pastels by Laura Coombs Hills. Displeased with the way pastel worked on paper, she considered her early attempts unsuccessful.[1] During a visit to Japan in 1937, Verner studied ink painting with a Japanese master and explored the idea of applying the pastel crayons to raw silk glued to a wooden support. Her method was to draw on the silk while it was still wet, which allowed her to work in modulated layers of color. Once the silk had dried, she added the final touches. She called the process Vernercolor.

Pastel became Verner's favored medium as it ideally combined the elements of drawing and painting. The new medium led to new motifs. Although flower women had appeared as accessories in her etchings, they became the primary focus of her pastels. Their animated gestures and colorful costumes made them attractive subjects for the artist. She turned to other subjects in the 1940s: live oaks draped in moss; tall cypress trees standing in abandoned rice preserves; rural cabins with blue doors and windows; and the streets of Charleston—always a favorite theme. During this decade, her works filled with light, enlivened by brilliant color; her pastels developed a rich, creamy touch. *Oak Grove/Middleton* dates from this period.

The oaks at Middleton Place inspired a number of evocative compositions. To Verner, the trees were a metaphor for the land. She wrote:

> This Low-Country is a land full of song and story, a sad land, certainly robbed as it has been of its splendor, but to the artist it is a paradise for it has lost nothing of its beauty. Its loveliness still remains, and perhaps possesses a greater harmony than in the days of its glory. Did the gnarled and hoary live oaks, draped in their solemn moss, play the part of a setting for that golden age as well as they now play the role of silent witnesses of the past, facing each other in long lines, an abandoned avenue with only a pile of overgrown ruins at the end to show where the Great House once stood?[2]

NRS

EVERETT LONGLEY WARNER (1877–1963)

Everett Warner grew up in Washington, D.C. and received his first art instruction at the Art Students League while still in high school. Upon graduation, he began a five-year stint as the art critic for the *Washington Evening Star*. Warner continued his studies in 1900 at the Art Students League in New York under George Bridgeman and in Paris at the Académie Julien. From 1903 until 1908, he traveled and painted in Europe and in the United States, exhibiting watercolors, pastels, etchings, and oil paintings in competitive shows and receiving many awards. He joined the art colony of Old Lyme in 1909 and spent the next fifteen years as a part-time resident. The tonalist concerns of Warner's earlier period gave way at this time to the bright, vibrant impressionism characteristic of the Old Lyme group. The work he painted there formed the basis of his reputation as a landscape artist.

After serving as a camouflage artist for the U.S. Navy during World War I, Warner returned to New York and directed his attention to urban scenes. Later in life, his reputation was as a painter of New York. On a 1923 sketching trip to Melrose, Florida, Warner fell in love with a young nurse whom he subsequently married. To support his new family, he took a teaching job at the Carnegie Institute of Technology in Pittsburgh and painted realist views of the steel mills, the railroad, and other industrial sites in his spare time. Recalled to the Navy at age sixty-five, he served as Chief Civilian Aide, Ship Camouflage until 1945 and then moved permanently to New Hampshire, where he continued to paint until his death in 1963.

Throughout his career, Warner painted both impressionist landscapes and haunting tonalist works. *Moonlight, Melrose, Florida*, with its soft greens and mauves, is typical of his tonalist compositions, but takes on an exotic quality because of the tropical vegetation. It was probably painted during his 1923 sketching trip to Melrose, although it could also have been painted at a later date, perhaps on a visit to his wife's family. Warner painted at least three other pastels of the same wooded area, but the trees are viewed from different angles; a cabin appears in one, suggesting that he may have stayed there during his trip.

NRS

Moonlight, Melrose, Florida, circa 1923
Pastel on paper, 26 x 20 inches
Collection of Delores and Allen Lastinger

Docks, New Orleans, circa 1889
Watercolor on paper, 9 x 12 inches
Signed lower right: *P. Woltze*

The son of painter and professor Berthold Woltze, Peter Woltze was born in Halberstadt, Germany. While his career encompassed activity in Europe and America, few details of his life are known. He was an accomplished watercolorist specializing in architectural subjects, though several portraits have been attributed to him as well. In Germany, Woltze studied and worked in Weimar, Karlsruhe, and Munich, before moving on to similar pursuits in Venice and Rome. From 1886 to 1900, Woltze lived in Milwaukee, Wisconsin. He apparently traveled to New Orleans in 1889 as evidenced by a number of views of the city, including *Docks, New Orleans*, and also to Mexico in 1899. Following his extended stay in America, Woltze returned to Germany, settling in Frankfurt. He resided there until 1907, when he moved back to Weimar and lived out the remainder of his days.

Woltze's deft skill with the watercolor medium is seen in both the sum and parts of this complex outdoor genre scene. An animated view of a bustling commercial port, *Docks, New Orleans* is layered with detailed activity in the fore-, middle-, and background. Multiple figures, animals, architecture, and landscape elements enliven the panorama. The structured composition is fluid and assured in its conception and is thereby characteristic of Woltze's other known works. His art is represented in the West Bend Art Museum and Milwaukee Art Museum collections.

VAL

MABEL MAY WOODWARD (1877–1945)

Best known for her summer garden and beach scenes painted along the New England shore, Mabel May Woodward was born in Providence, Rhode Island and received her initial art training at the Rhode Island School of Design. She advanced her education at the Art Students League in New York City under Frank DuMond and William Merritt Chase, and also studied with Arthur Wesley Dow, Charles Woodbury, and Charles Hawthorne. In 1900, Woodward returned to her native city and joined the faculty at the Rhode Island School of Design, where she taught for many years.

Like most plein air painters, Woodward traveled constantly in search of subject matter. In addition to summers along the New England coast, she visited and painted in France, Italy, and Holland. She also made at least one trip to the South, stopping in Charleston, New Orleans, and St. Augustine. Though Woodward rarely dated her scenes, she usually identified their location in the titles. *Flower Ladies, Charleston* is one of a group of pastels, charcoals, and oils—mostly outdoor scenes of sun-struck buildings and rural cabins—that record her stay in the Lowcountry. Although the pastel is devoid of background, an outdoor setting is suggested by the light spilling across the figures and by the high-keyed palette.

Woodward was likely drawn to the subject by the work of Elizabeth O'Neill Verner, whose depictions of the city's African American flower vendors were widely admired during the late 1930s and 1940s. Though the women were the primary focus of Verner's paintings, they were of secondary interest to Woodward. When figures appear in her scenes, they are typically diminutive, greatly overshadowed by their environment. While this example lacks Woodward's usual attention to setting, the bold brushwork and bright palette are characteristic of her distinct style, described in 1938 as "a kind of impressionism . . . or a development of impressionism to a more descriptive painting."[1]

NRS

Flower Ladies, Charleston, circa 1935-1940
Pastel on paper, 11 x 15¾ inches
Signed lower left: *M. Woodward.*

Old Brick, Edisto Island, S.C., View of Creek, circa 1915
Pastel on paper, 20 x 25 inches
Signed lower right: *G. Wright*

GEORGE HAND WRIGHT (1872–1951)

Once described as "the undisputed top illustrator in the nation," George Hand Wright was born to a Quaker family in Fox Chase, Pennsylvania.[1] The son of a blacksmith, he studied at the Spring Garden Institute and the Academy of Fine Arts in Philadelphia and in Paris and Munich, before settling in New York City. By the turn of the century, he had established himself there as a genre painter and illustrator.

In 1907, Wright moved permanently to Westport, Connecticut and was a founder of the art colony that developed in that community a few years later. From 1900 until his death in 1951, he worked as a freelance illustrator for various publications, including *Harper's, The Century, Scribner's*, and, in later years, *The Saturday Evening Post*. Simultaneously, he painted genre subjects—primarily outdoor scenes—in Connecticut, New York City, the South, and other places, including Canada and Europe, on story assignments. Wright was a member of many important art organizations and exhibited at the National Academy of Design, Salmagundi Club, Grand Central Galleries, and other venues. His work was widely admired, especially by his fellow artists, who considered him one of the finest talents of his generation.

Wright achieved his earliest success in the 1890s, with a series of oils depicting bashful suitors in awkward situations, but he is chiefly admired for his illustrations. Like John Sloan, Everett Shinn, and other artist-reporters, he approached his sketchbooks as diaries, making finished illustrations from on-the-spot drawings. Many of the artist's sketches were reproduced directly in the magazines as coverage for accompanying articles.[2] Wright is known to have made no distinction between these illustrations and the fine arts prints, watercolors, and pastels he created independent of magazine commissions.

Wright's travels in the South are not documented, and his work is rarely dated. He appears, however, to have visited South Carolina on at least one occasion, in 1915, when he recorded aspects of African American life in Beaufort, a small coastal town seventy miles south of Charleston. Watercolors of *Zig Zag Alley, Chalmers Street,* and related locales suggest that Wright began his trip in Charleston and then traveled to Beaufort by boat, stopping at Edisto Island to paint a series of pastels, including *Old Brick, Edisto Island, S.C., View of Creek*. Old Brick—constructed in 1725 of brick imported from Boston—was the focal point of a 325-acre cotton plantation located beside Russell Creek, west of the North Fork Edisto River. At the time of Wright's visit, the house had fallen into disrepair. A fire in 1929 destroyed all but the shell, and the building is now a ruin.

The large size of this pastel, as well as the completeness of the image, suggest that Wright envisioned it as more than a casual sketch. Rendered on gray paper, the pastel reveals a richer, more diverse treatment than seen in Wright's other works in the medium, usually characterized by a sparer application. He applied his crayons in a painterly fashion and incorporated the tone of the paper into his design. The result is a work that captures the animated qualities within this peaceful scene.

The Veterans, 1993
Watercolor on paper, 16¾ x 14¾ inches
Signed lower left: *SS Young*
Inscribed lower center: *1st Composition Study/Greenville South/Carolina*
Inscribed lower right: *The Veterans/Memorial Day 1993/V F W*

One of the foremost realist painters working today, Stephen Scott Young strives to capture an exacting sense of realism in colloquial scenes of everyday, small-town life. Born in Hawaii, he spent his youth in Gainesville, Florida, where he attended Flagler College, followed by three years at the Ringling School of Art in Sarasota. Young initially studied printmaking in art school, but began experimenting with watercolor in 1976. He now primarily employs watercolor and drybrush, working occasionally in tempera or oil. An avid student of the work of historical artists, he admires the work of Old Masters such as Vermeer, Caravaggio, Rembrandt, David, and Gérôme. Ultimately, however, the art of American masters, such as Homer, Hassam, Sargent, and Wyeth, provided even more important precedents in shaping Young's aesthetic.

Young visited Harbour Island in the Bahamas in 1987, a trip that inspired him to adopt a new direction. It was there that he began recording African American subjects, which has been the focus of his oeuvre ever since. Each work Young undertakes is a visual representation of the unique personal relationship he develops with the model.

In 1993, an exhibition of his art traveled to Greenville, South Carolina, and Young was subsequently commissioned by the Greenville County Museum of Art to execute a series of works titled *Portrait of Greenville*. *The Veterans* is one of the first studies the artist did in preparation for a large watercolor of the same title, now in the museum's permanent collection. The scene depicts two veterans, Dewitt Jackson and Willie Norris, sitting outside a white clapboard VFW hall in a local neighborhood on Memorial Day. The artist worked while the men reminisced about their World War II experiences. The composition of the final painting—which depicts the scene from a head-on view, with both figures sitting on opposing sides of the porch engaged in conversation— underwent considerable revision from this study.

This watercolor is executed in a liberated style with a wet-on-wet technique that Young often employs for on-site preparatory studies. There is a sense of immediacy in these watercolors that is not evident in his more controlled large compositions, which are painstakingly created by the building up of layers of pigment.

The Veterans is not the only composition to depict a flag or address themes of patriotism in Young's work. One of his most well known compositions, *Promised* (1991; private collection) portrays a young girl gazing down at a flag in her lap. The son of a wounded Vietnam veteran, Young is keenly attuned to the dignity of military service. While this watercolor references the idea of patriotism, its central focus is the characterizations of the two figures and the formal elements of the composition, notably the effect of light on the drapery of the flag and the architecture. These aspects of the work highlight Young's artistic mastery and unparalleled technical proficiency.

137

annotations

The following citations reference both specific endnotes to catalogue essays, as well as recommended resources on particular artists. A select bibliography presented at the end of these documentations offers suggested readings on works on paper and the development of the European-American artistic traditions of drawing, watercolor, and gouache.

DRAWING THE SOUTH

[1] Robert M. Hicklin, Jr., "Blackberry Winter," *Calm in the Shadow of the Palmetto and Magnolia: Southern Art from the Charleston Renaissance Gallery* (Charleston, South Carolina: Charleston Renaissance Gallery, 2003), 2-3.

[2] I suspect that these drawings are comfortably at home in Charleston where, on my first visit there many years ago, I read the obituary of a prominent citizen who was described as a "relative newcomer to Charleston, his family having lived here for only three generations."

[3] Drawing authority, former director, and curator emeritus of the Arkansas Art Center Townsend Wolfe offers the following definition: "A drawing is any unique work of art on paper." The key word is unique. Included in this definition would be images done in graphite, charcoal, pen and ink, crayon, and metal point, as well as paintings in watercolor and pastel. Multiple prints, with the possible exception of monotypes, would be excluded. This definition fails in that some works of art, clearly drawings, have been done on cave walls, blackboards, and canvas.

[4] For a fuller understanding of the watercolor medium, I recommend the following volumes. Cohn, Marjorie B. *Wash and Gouache: A Study of the Materials of Watercolor*. Cambridge, Massachussetts: Harvard University, Fogg Art Museum, 1977. This is a standard reference; unfortunately, the illustrative exhibition, for which it was the accompanying text, is no longer available. Also: Reed, Sue Welsh and Carol Troyen. *Awash in Color: Homer, Sargent, and the Great American Watercolor*. New York: Little, Brown & Company, 1999. This publication, also an exhibition catalogue, contains beautiful color reproductions and a concise chapter on the watercolor medium and paper.

[5] Martha R. Severens, *Alice Ravenel Huger Smith: An Artist, a Place and a Time* (Charleston, South Carolina: Carolina Art Association/Gibbes Museum of Art, 1993), 45.

[6] H. S. Halbert and T. H. Ball, *The Creek War of 1813 and 1814*, rev. ed., ed. Frank L. Owsley (Tuscaloosa: University of Alabama Press, 1995). This historical account was originally published in 1895 by Donohue & Henneberry of Chicago.

[7] As described by Catlin on a companion sheet to his 1852 sketch, *Tol-lee: Cherokee*. The accompanying inscription reads: *184/Cherokee/Tol-lee (__) Chief of a Band, Civilized/and half caste./A tribe of 20,000, chiefly civilized and/ agricultural. All removed by President/Jackson, to the Arkansas, 700. miles W. of the/Mississippi. They formerly lived in the State/of Georgia.*

[8] Patricia E. Phagan, ed., *The American Scene and the South: Painting and Works on Paper, 1930-1946* (Athens: Georgia Museum of Art, University of Georgia, 1996). This pioneer publication contains informative chapters covering Southern American Scene painting in Alabama by William Eiland; in Louisiana and Mississippi by Richard Cox; in South Carolina by Martha Severens; and in Georgia, North Carolina, and Virginia by Phagan.

[9] Dr. Edmund Taylor, nephew of the artist, personal communication with the author.

[10] Dale Volberg Reed, "Society for the Preservation of Spirituals," *The South Carolina Encyclopedia*, ed. Walter Edgar (Columbia: University of South Carolina Press, 2006), 888.

[11] Stewart Emory Tolnay and E. M. Beck, *A Festival of Violence: An Analysis of Southern Lynchings, 1882-1930* (Champaign: University of Illinois Press, 1995).

[12] William Faulkner, *Requiem for a Nun* (New York: Random House, 1951). "The past is never dead. It's not even past." Said by Gavin Stevens, Act 1, Scene 3.

[13] Clarence John Laughlin, *Ghosts along the Mississippi: An Essay in the Poetic Interpretation of Louisiana's Plantation Architecture*, rev. ed. (New York: Bonanza Books, 1961).

[14] Paul Cummings, "A Discipline Aborning: Twentieth Century American Drawing Studies," *Drawing* XIV (September-October 1992): 52-56.

ABBOT

[1] As quoted in Pamela Gilbert, *John Abbot: Birds, Butterflies and Other Wonders* (London: Natural History Museum, 1998), 117.

[2] Ibid., 118.

Additional Sources:

Rogers-Price, Vivian. *John Abbot in Georgia: The Vision of a Naturalist Artist*. Exhibition catalogue. Madison, Georgia: Madison-Morgan Cultural Center, 1983.

Simpson, Jr., Marcus B. "Artistic Sources for John Abbot's Watercolor Drawings of American Birds," *Archives of Natural History* 20 (1993): 197-212.

Simpson, Jr., Marcus B. "The Artist-Naturalist John Abbot (1751-ca. 1840): Contributions to the Ornithology of the Southeastern United States," *North Carolina Historical Review* 3 (July 1984): 347-390.

ARTHUR

Bailey, N. Louise, et al. *Biographical Directory of the South Carolina Senate*. Columbia: University of South Carolina Press, 1986.

Lucas, Marion B. *Sherman and the Burning of Columbia*. Columbia: University of South Carolina Press, 2002.

Simms, William Gilmore. *A City Laid Waste: The Capture, Sack and Destruction of the City of Columbia*, edited with an introduction by David Aiken. Columbia: University of South Carolina Press, 2005.

South Carolinian (Columbia, South Carolina), May 18, 1847, 2-3.

BEATTIE

Beattie, Drew. *George Beattie: Portraits and Landscapes from the 1950s to the 1990s*. Exhibition catalogue. Atlanta: Swan Coach House Gallery, 2001.

Bishop, Isabel. *George Beattie*. Exhibition catalogue. New York: Hirschl & Adler Galleries, 1960.

Fox, Catherine. "Faces, Places Reflect Beattie Genius," *Atlanta Journal-Constitution*, November 9, 2001.

BENSON

The Art of Frank W. Benson: American Impressionist. Exhibition catalogue. Salem: Massachussetts: Peabody Essex Museum, 2000.

Frank W. Benson: A Retrospective. Exhibition catalogue. New York: Berry-Hill Galleries, Inc., 1989.

BERNATH

Art for the New Collector IV. Exhibition catalogue. New York: Spanierman Gallery, LLC, 2005.

www.georgeglazer.com/prints

BIDDLE

Biddle, George. *An American Artist's Story*. Boston: Little, Brown & Co., 1939.

Severens, Martha R. *The Charleston Renaissance*. Spartanburg, South Carolina: Saraland Press, 1998.

BIGGS

"Biggs Paintings of Local Scenes Exhibited," *A Guide to Historical Salem* 4 (Winter 1998-1999).

BLACKWELL

[1] Quoted from artist's statement in Frank Thomson, *Tarleton Blackwell*. Exhibition catalogue (Asheville, North Carolina: Asheville Art Museum, 1992), unpaginated.

Additional sources:

Leach, Mark Richard. *Tarleton Blackwell*. Charlotte, North Carolina: Mint Museum of Art, 1992.

O'Hara, Catherine L. *Tarleton Blackwell: Greatest Show of Hogs*. Exhibition catalogue. Cincinnati, Ohio: Taft Museum, 1993.

Sokolitz, Roberta. *Tarleton Blackwell's Southern Campaign: The Swine Project*. Exhibition catalogue. Charleston, South Carolina: Hicklin Galleries, LLC/The Charleston Renaissance Gallery, 2005.

BROOKE

[1] Andrew J. Consentino and Henry H. Glassie, *The Capital Image: Painters in Washington, 1800-1915* (Washington, D.C.: Smithsonian Institution Press, 1983), 201.

[2] Richard Norris Brooke, "*Record of Work . . . Since my departure for Paris in 1878.*" Manuscript. No. 305:110, Smithsonian American Art Museum Library, Washington, D.C.

BRUCE

[1] William C. Agee and Barbara Rose, *Patrick Henry Bruce, American Modernist: A Catalogue Raisonne* (New York: Museum of Modern Art, 1979), 43.

[2] Ibid., 52.

[3] William Styron, *This Quiet Dust* (New York: Random House, 1982), 49.

CALYO

[1] I am grateful to John Magill, Curator, Williams Research Center of the Historic New Orleans Collection for identifying the Odd Fellows Hall and other buildings, and for directing me to the Mondelli/Bennett aquatint, *New Orleans, Taken from the Opposite Side, a Short Distance Above the Middle or Picayune Ferry*. See http://www.nypl.org/research/chss/spe/art/prints/exhibits/cities/captions/image34.html.

Additional Sources:

Obituary, *New York Tribune*, December 14, 1884.

Patterson, Marilyn Sloane. "Nicolino Calyo and His Paintings of the Great Fire of New York, December 16th and 17th, 1835," *American Art Journal* XIV, no. 2 (Spring 1982): 4-22.

CATLIN

[1] Peter H. Hassrick, *Drawings of the North American Indians* (New York: Doubleday & Company, 1984), x.

[2] Ibid., xxv.

Additional source:

Gurney, George and Therese Thau Heyman, eds. *George Catlin and His Indian Gallery*. Exhibition catalogue Washington, D.C.: Smithsonian American Art Museum, 2003.

CHAMPNEY

[1] Edward King, "A Ramble in Virginia," *Scribner's Magazine* (April 1874): 671.

[2] Edward King, *The Great South* (Hartford, Connecticut: American Publishing Company, 1875), 591. This drawing is one of about 240 drawings from "The Great South" series by Champney, presently held in the collection of the Lilly Library, Indiana University, Bloomington. This information is from research conducted by Sue Rainey. See Sue Rainey to Caroline Igou, December 26, 2005, Charleston Renaissance Gallery archive.

Additional source:

McKay, Robert J., et al. *James Wells Champney, 1843-1903*. Exhibition catalogue. Deerfield, Massachussetts: Hilson Gallery, Deerfield Academy, 1965.

CLEMENTS

Delehanty, Randolph. *Art in the American South: Works from the Ogden Collection*. Baton Rouge, Louisiana: Louisiana State University Press, 1996.

CRONAU

Bourque, Monique. "The Register of the Collection of Rudolf Cronau: 1858-1930." Balch Institute for Ethnic Studies, Philadelphia, Pennsylvania.

Wunderlich, Gerold M. *Rudolf Cronau, 1855-1939: Topographical Views of America*. Exhibition catalogue. New York: Gerold Wunderlich & Company, 1993.

DODGE

Pisano, Ronald. *William de Leftwich Dodge: Impressions Home and Abroad*. Exhibition catalogue. New York: Beacon Hill Fine Art, 1998.

DOUGAL

Groce, George C. and David H. Wallace. *New-York Historical Society's Dictionary of American Sculptors & Engravers 1564-1860*. New Haven, Connecticut: Yale University Press, 1957.

Hughes, Edan Milton. *Artists in California, 1786-1940*, 3rd ed. Sacramento, California: Crocker Art Museum, 2002.

DUNLAP

[1] As quoted in Mary Lynn Kotz, "Bill Dunlap's Northern Offensive," *Museum and Arts Washington*, volume 5 (March/April 1989): 70.

[2] William Dunlap to Ruth Stevens Appelhof, "An Interview," in *William Dunlap: Re-Constructed Re-Collections*. Exhibition catalogue (Roanoke, Virginia: Art Museum of Western Virginia, 1992), 2.

[3] Bill Kovach, "William Dunlap: Painting in the Southern Narrative Tradition," in *Dunlap: Re-Constructed*, 8.

Additional sources:

William Dunlap. Jackson: University Press of Mississippi, 2006. Essays by Julia Reed and J. Richard Gruber.

Williams, Jay. *What Dogs Dream: Paintings and Works on Paper by William Dunlap*. Exhibition catalogue. Augusta, Georgia: Morris Museum of Art, 2006.

ENGLISH

The Rediscovery of Frank F. English: Bucks County Landscape Artist. Exhibition catalogue. Lahaska, Pennsylvania: Bianco Gallery, 1988.

FALCONER

[1] See entries on Falconer in Sue Welsh Reed and Carol Troyen, *Awash in Color: Homer, Sargent, and the Great American Watercolor* (Boston: Museum of Fine Arts, 1993), 24-27; and Linda S. Ferber, "Our Mr. John M. Falconer" in *Brooklyn Before the Bridge, Paintings from the Long Island Historical Society* (Brooklyn: Brooklyn Museum, 1982), 16, 18.

[2] Reed and Troyen, *Awash in Color*, 25, 26.

FANTUZZO

[1] Linda Fantuzzo, as quoted in "Linda Fantuzzo Shows Italian Paintings at Morris Gallery," undated, unknown newspaper. Charleston Renaissance Gallery archive.

Additional sources:

Fleming, Elizabeth A. in *Framing a Vision: Landscapes by Linda Fantuzzo and Manning Williams*. Exhibition catalogue. Charleston, South Carolina: Gibbes Museum of Art, 2004.

Linda Fantuzzo: Paintings. Exhibition catalogue. Charleston: Gibbes Museum of Art, 1992.

Sokolitz, Roberta. *Edges: The Paintings of Linda Fantuzzo*. Exhibition catalogue. Charleston, South Carolina: Hicklin Galleries, LLC/Charleston Renaissance Gallery, 2008.

FITZPATRICK

[1] May Belle Gay, *John Kelly Fitzpatrick: Retrospective Exhibition*. Exhibition catalogue (Montgomery, Alabama: Montgomery Museum of Fine Arts, 1970), 5.

[2] Dixie Art Colony papers, as quoted in Christine Neal, et al., *A Symphony of Color: The World of Kelly Fitzpatrick, 1888-1953*. Exhibition catalogue (Montgomery, Alabama: Montgomery Museum of Fine Arts, 1991), 50.

[3] John Kelly Fitzpatrick, November 10, 1945, as quoted in Neal, *Symphony of Color,* 35.

FLAGG

Meyer, Susan E. *James Montgomery Flagg.* New York: Watson-Guptill Publications, 1974.

GRAHAM

Samuels, Peggy and Harold. *Illustrated Biographical Encyclopedia of Artists of the American West.* Garden City, New York: Doubleday, 1976.

Hughes, Edan Milton. *Artists in California: 1786-1940*, 2nd ed. San Francisco: Hughes Publishing Company, 1989.

HALSEY

[1] Jack A. Morris, Jr., *William M. Halsey: Retrospective* (Greenville, South Carolina: Greenville County Museum of Art, 1972), 24, 75.

Additional sources:

Severens, Martha R. *William Halsey.* Greenville, South Carolina: Greenville County Museum of Art, 1999.

Wright, Caroline Cobb. *William Halsey: Mastery of the Modern.* Exhibition catalogue. Charleston, South Carolina: Hicklin Galleries LLC/Charleston Renaissance Gallery, 2006.

HERRING

[1] Clint Herring, interviews with the author, August 6 and August 16, 2007.

[2] Joanne Moore, "The Simple Life," *The Artist's Magazine*, vol. 21 (July 2004): 48.

HOLLINGSWORTH

Cole, Hunter. "William Hollingsworth: An Artist of Joy and Sadness," *Mississippi History Now* (November 2005), http://mshistory.k12.ms.us/index.php?s=article&id+37.

Hollingsworth, Jane, ed. *Hollingsworth: The Man, the Artist, and His Work.* Jackson: University Press of Mississippi, 1981.

Welty, Eudora. *On William Hollingsworth, Jr.* Jackson: University Press of Mississippi, 2002.

HÖLZLHUBER

Buchanan, Thomas C. *Black Life on the Mississippi: Slaves, Free Blacks, and the Western Steamboat World*. Chapel Hill: University of North Carolina Press, 2004.

Feest, Christian S. and Sylvia S. Kasprycki. *Peoples of the Twilight: European Views of Native Minnesota*. Afton, Minnesota: Afton Historical Society Press, 1999.

Maser, Edward A. *The American Sketchbooks of Franz Hölzlhuber: An Austrian Visits America in 1856-1860*. Exhibition catalogue. Lawrence: University of Kansas Museum of Art, 1959.

"Sketches from Northwestern America and Canada: A Portfolio of Water Colors by Franz Hölzlhuber," *American Heritage* 16 (June 1965): 49-64.

HULL

Norwood, Malcolm M., Virginia McGehee Elias and William S. Haynie. *The Art of Marie Hull*. Jackson: University Press of Mississippi, 1975.

HUTTY

[1] Boyd Saunders and Ann McAden. *Alfred Hutty and the Charleston Renaissance* (Orangeburg, South Carolina: Sandlapper Publishing Company, 1990), 13.

[2] Ibid., 27.

Additional source:

Severens, Martha R. *The Charleston Renaissance*. Spartanburg, South Carolina: Saraland Press, 1998.

LAW

[1] Robert Henri, *The Art Spirit*, Margery Ryerson, ed. (1923; reprint, New York: Dover Books, 1984), 218.

[2] *Journal and Carolina Spartan*, (Spartanburg, South Carolina), March 2, 1937, as quoted in Zan Schuweiler Daab, *Margaret Law: Painter of Southern Life*. Exhibition catalogue (Spartanburg, South Carolina: Spartanburg County Museum of Art, 1999), unpaginated.

[3] "Fine Exhibits Are Being Shown at Museum," *Montgomery Advertiser*, April 1947, Gibbes Museum of Art archives, Charleston, South Carolina.

LAZZELL

Bridges, Robert, Kristina Olsen and Janet Snyder, *Blanche Lazzell: The Life and Work of an American Modernist* (Morgantown: West Virginia University Press, 2004).

Shapiro, Barbara Stern, *From Paris to Provincetown: Blanche Lazzell and the Color Woodcut*. Exhibition catalogue (Boston: MFA Publications/Museum of Fine Arts, 2002).

MANIGAULT

Middleton Manigault: Visionary Modernist. Exhibition catalogue. New York: Hollis Taggart Galleries and the Columbus Museum of Art, Ohio, 2002.

McCALLUM

Halsey, William. "The First Shot and the Longest Siege," *Ford Times*, March 1961: 6-9.

Kefalos, Roberta Sokolitz. *William Halsey and Corrie McCallum: Now and Then*. Exhibition catalogue. Charleston, South Carolina: Gibbes Museum of Art, 1989.

Mack, Angela. "Corrie McCallum: A Life in Art," *Corrie McCallum: A Life in Art.* Exhibition catalogue. Charleston, South Carolina: Gibbes Museum of Art, 1995.

Severens, Martha R. *Corrie McCallum: Take Note.* Greenville, South Carolina: Greenville County Museum of Art, 2004.

MURRAY

Biography, Morris Museum of Art archives, Augusta, Georgia.

NEWMAN

[1] "New Names Enliven Morton Watercolor Show," *Art Digest* XV, no. 1 (October 1940): 19.

[2] Ibid.

[3] Obituary, *New York Times*, January 27, 1982.

[4] Estate auction catalogue (North Bethesda, Maryland: C. G. Sloan, 1997), 25-27.

OELSCHIG

Delorme, Harry H., Jr. and Pamela D. King. *Looking Back: Art in Savannah 1900-1960.* Savannah, Georgia: Telfair Museum of Art, 1996.

From Darkness to Light: The Paintings of Savannah's Augusta Oelschig. Exhibition catalogue. Savannah, Georgia: Telfair Museum of Art, 2000.

PITTMAN

Hobson Pittman Retrospective Exhibition: His Work Since 1920. Exhibition catalogue. Raleigh: North Carolina Museum of Art, 1963.

The World of Hobson Pittman: A Retrospective Exhibition. Exhibition catalogue. University Park: Museum of Art, Pennsylvania State University, 1972.

RICHARDS

[1] Elizabeth F. Ellet, *The Women of the American Revolution*, vol. 2 (New York: Baker and Scribner, 1850), 86.

Additional sources:

Drawings: T. Addison Richards. Exhibition catalogue. New York: Washburn Gallery, 1974.

Kefalos, Roberta Sokolitz. "Thomas Addison Richards: The Search for the Picturesque and the Landscape of the South." Master's thesis, University of Pittsburgh, 1996.

Koch, Mary Levin. "The Romance of American Landscape: The Art of Thomas Addison Richards," *Georgia Museum of Art Bulletin* 8, no. 2 (Winter 1983): 5-36.

SAWYIER

[1] Arthur F. Jones, *The Art of Paul Sawyier* (Lexington: University Press of Kentucky, 1976), 94, 98.

Additional sources:

Jillson, Willard Rouse. *Paul Sawyier: American Artist 1865-1917, A Biographical Sketch.* Frankfort, Kentucky: Blue Grass Press, 1971.

Jillson, Willard Rouse. *Paul Sawyier and His Paintings, Centennial Exhibition (1865-1965).* Exhibition catalogue. Louisville, Kentucky: J. B. Speed Memorial Museum, 1965.

SHANNON

[1] Charles Shannon correspondence, April 10, 1938, as quoted in *Charles Shannon, Paintings of the South*. Exhibition catalogue (New York: Jacques Seligman and Company, 1938).

Additional sources:

Charles Shannon: Paintings and Drawings. Exhibition catalogue. Montgomery, Alabama: ArtSouth, Inc., 1981.

Eiland, William U., "Picturing the Unvictorious: The Southern Scene in Alabama." *The American Scene and the South, Paintings and Works on Paper, 1930-1946.* Exhibition catalogue. Athens: Georgia Museum of Art, University of Georgia, 1996.

SHAW

[1] For this group of paintings and sketches, see *A Paradise of Riches: Joshua Shaw and the Southern Frontier* (Greenville, South Carolina: Greenville County Museum of Art, 2008); and Martha R. Severens. "The Southern Sojourn of Joshua Shaw," *American Art Review* XXI, no. 5 (September-October 2008). Special thanks to Martha Severens, Greenville County Museum of Art Curator, for sharing her expertise on the artist and these works with me.

[2] Shaw's manuscript autobiography is discussed in "Joshua Shaw, Artist and Inventor: The Early History of the Copper Percussion Cup," *Scientific American*, August 7, 1869, http://www.researchpress.co.uk/firearms/ignition/shaw.htm.

[3] Miriam Carroll Woods' master's thesis, "Joshua Shaw (1776-1860): A Study of the Artist and His Paintings" (University of California, Los Angeles, 1971) is the most comprehensive publication on the artist's life and work.

[4] Gloria-Gilda Deak, *Picturing America*, 1497-1899 (Princeton, New Jersey: Princeton University Press, 1988), vol. I: 213-214; vol. II: nos. 315.1-20.

[5] Shaw manuscript account of the Natural Bridge, Charleston Renaissance Gallery, Charleston, South Carolina.

[6] *Scientific American*, 1869.

ALICE SMITH

[1] *Alice Ravenel Huger Smith of Charleston, South Carolina, an Appreciation on the Occasion of her Eightieth Birthday* (Charleston, South Carolina: privately published, 1956), cat. nos. 281, 298, 321, 560.

[2] Martha R. Severens, *Alice Ravenel Huger Smith: An Artist, a Place and a Time* (Charleston, South Carolina: Carolina Art Association/Gibbes Museum of Art, 1993), 45.

[3] Letter from Alice R. Huger Smith to Mr. Millsaps, April 19, 1939, published in the *Carolinian* (May 1939): 7.

Additional Sources:

McCormack, Helen Gardner. "Alice Ravenel Huger Smith: An Appreciation." *Retrospective Exhibition of the Work of Alice Ravenel Huger Smith*. Charleston, South Carolina: Carolina Art Association, 1947.

Sokolitz, Roberta. *The Sound of the Wind in the Pines: The Poetic Vision of Alice Ravenel Huger Smith*. Exhibition catalogue. Charleston, South Carolina: Carolina Galleries, 2002.

XANTHUS SMITH

Fisher, James Louis. "Xanthus Smith: Civil War Painter." Master's thesis, University of Delaware, 1982.

Mary, Xanthus, and Russell Smith Family Papers, 1826-1954. Archives of American Art, Smithsonian Institution, Washington, D.C.

STEPHENS

[1] As quoted in Ann Barton Brown, *Alice Barber Stephens: A Pioneer Woman Illustrator*. Exhibition catalogue (Chadds Ford, Pennsylvania: Brandywine River Museum, 1984), 8.

[2] Ibid., 13.

Additional source:

Rubinstein, Charlotte Streifer. *American Women Artists from Early Indian Times to the Present*. Boston: G. K. Hall and Co., 1982.

LESTER STEVENS

[1] Sheila Seaman and Robert L. Merriam, *W. Lester Stevens, N.A. 1888-1969* (Greenfield, Massachusetts: Greenfield Community College Foundation, 1977), 13.

WILL HENRY STEVENS

Devree, Howard, *New York Times*, March 2, 1941, as quoted in *Will Henry Stevens*. Exhibition catalogue. Greenville, South Carolina: Greenville County Museum of Art, 1987.

Levin, Gail and Marianne Lorenz. *Themes & Improvisation: Kandinsky & the American Avant-Garde 1912-1950*. Boston: Little Brown, 1992.

Lorenz, Marianne. "Will Henry Stevens: Abstract Landscapes and Non-Objectives: Mature Work 1938-1949." Asheville, North Carolina: Blue Spiral Gallery, undated, unpaginated.

SYKES

Laufer, Marilyn, et al. *The Spirit of the Modern: Drawings and Graphics by Maltby Sykes*. Exhibition Catalogue. Athens: Georgia Museum of Art, University of Georgia, 2004.

TAYLOR

Burgess, Lana Ann. "Anna Heyward Taylor: 'Her Work which is of Enduring Quality Will Remain to Attest to Her Reputation as an Artist and Her Generosity as a Citizen.'" Master's thesis, University of South Carolina, 1994.

Dennison, Mariea Caudill. "Art of the American South, 1915-1945: Picturing the Past, Portending Regionalism." Ph.D. diss., University of Illinois at Urbana-Champaign, 2000.

Severens, Martha R. *Anna Heyward Taylor: Printmaker*. Exhibition catalogue. Greenville, South Carolina: Greenville County Museum of Art, 1987.

VERNER

[1] David Hamilton, grandson of the artist, telephone conversation with the author, July 2006.

[2] Elizabeth O'Neill Verner, *Prints and Impressions of Charleston*. (Columbia, South Carolina: Bostick and Thornley, 1939), unpaginated.

Additional sources:

Myers, Lynn Robertson. *Mirror of Time: Elizabeth O'Neill Verner's Charleston*. Exhibition catalogue. Columbia: McKissick Museums, University of South Carolina, 1983.

Severens, Martha R. *The Charleston Renaissance*. Spartanburg, SC: Saraland Press, 1998.

WARNER

Fusscas, Helen K. *A World Observed: The Art of Everett Longley Warner, 1877-1963*. Exhibtion catalogue. Old Lyme, Connecticut: Florence Griswold Museum, 1992.

WOODWARD

[1] Frank Sisson, *Providence* (Rhode Island) *Journal*, 1938, as quoted in Information Sheet, Mabel May Woodward, Bert Gallery, Providence, Rhode Island, unpaginated.

WRIGHT

[1] *Westporter-Herald*, 1920, as quoted in quoted in Dorothy Tarrant and John Tarrant, *A Community of Artists: Westport-Weston, 1900-1985* (Westport, Connecticut: Westport-Weston Arts Council, 1985), 11.

[2] Walt Reed, *The Illustrator in America, 1880-1980: A Century of Illustration* (New York: Madison Square Press, 1984), 83.

YOUNG

Leeds, Valerie Ann. *Stephen Scott Young: In the American Tradition*. Exhibition catalogue. Palm Beach, Florida: John H. Surovek Gallery and the Museum of Fine Arts, St. Petersburg, 1993.

SELECT BIBLIOGRAPHY

Bermingham, Ann. *Learning to Draw: Studies in the Cultural History of a Polite and Useful Art*. New Haven: Yale University Press/Paul Mellon Centre for Studies in British Art, 2000.

Bloch, E. Maurice. *Faces and Figures in American Drawings*. Exhibition catalogue. San Marino, California: Huntington Library Press, 1989.

Brewer, Philip L. and Theodore E. Stebbins, Jr. *Lines of Discovery: 225 Years of American Drawings*. Columbus, Georgia: Columbus Museum, 2006.

Cox, Richard. *Southern Works on Paper, 1900-1950*. Exhibition catalogue. Atlanta: Southern Arts Federation, 1981.

Coggins, Robert P. *Works on Paper from the Robert P. Coggins Collection of American Art*. Exhibition catalogue. Marietta, Georgia: Marietta-Cobb Fine Arts Center, 1984.

Davidson, Marshall B. *The Drawing of America: Eyewitnesses to History*. New York: Abrams, 1983.

Edidin, Stephen R., introduction. *Stories to Tell: Masterworks from the Kelly Collection of American Illustration*. Exhibition catalogue. New York: Dahesh Museum of Art, 2006.

Larson, Judy L., ed. *Graphic Arts & the South: Proceedings of the 1990 North American Print Conference*. Fayetteville: University of Arkansas Press, 1993.

Marzio, Peter C. *The Art Crusade: An Analysis of American Drawing Manuals, 1820-1860*. Washington, D.C.: Smithsonian Institution Press, 1976.

Stebbins, Jr., Theodore E. *American Master Drawings and Watercolors: A History of Works on Paper from Colonial Times to the Present*. New York: Harper & Row/The Drawing Society, 1976.

Wunderlich, Rudolf G., introduction, and Maria Naylor. *American Drawings, Pastels and Watercolors, Part One: Works of the Eighteenth and Early Nineteenth Centuries*. Exhibition catalogue. New York: Kennedy Galleries, 1967.

Wunderlich, Rudolf G., introduction, and Maria Naylor. *American Drawings, Pastels and Watercolors, Part Two: The Nineteenth Century; 1825-1890*. Exhibition catalogue. New York: Kennedy Galleries, 1968.

index